FRAMEWORK EDITION

Skills in
ENGLISH

3 R

Lindsay McNab

Imelda Pilgrim

Marian Slee

Literacy consultant: Jacqui Buckley

Heinemann

The authors and publishers would like to thank Bernadette Pearce for writing Section F – Words: spelling strategies and vocabulary. They would also like to extend grateful thanks to David Robinson for his work as Grammar Consultant on the series.

Heinemann Educational Publishers
Halley Court, Jordan Hill, Oxford, OX2 8EJ
Part of Harcourt Education

Heinemann is a registered trademark of Harcourt Education Limited

© Sections A–E: Lindsay McNab, Imelda Pilgrim, Marian Slee 2002
© Section F: Bernadette Pearce 2002

First published 2002
05   04   03
10   9   8   7   6   5   4   3

ISBN 0 435 19286 8

Designed by 320 Design. Produced by Gecko Ltd, Bicester, Oxon
Printed and bound in Italy by Printer Trento s.r.l

Picture research by Jennifer Johnson

Original illustrations © Heinemann Educational Publishers 2002

The Publishers would like to thank the following for permission to reproduce photographs on the pages noted.

BBC, pp.36, 38; Pearl Bucknell/Robert Harding, p.92; Camera Press, p.92; Corbis, pp.67, 124 and 125; M. Evans/Robert Harding, p.92; Express Syndication, pp.115 and 119; Melanie Friend, p.100; Ken Gilham/Robert Harding, p.92; Paula Glassman/Format, p.92; Honeywell, p.62; Hulton-Getty, pp.175 and 177; Press Association, p.177; Photodisc, pp.112 and 113; PYMCA, p.92; Peter Saunders, p.92; UPPA, pp.115 and 119; Vanderhast/Robert Harding, p.61.

Illustrations: Chris Brown, Abigail Conway, David Cuzik, Nick Duffy, Alice Englander, Teresa Flavin, Tony Forbes, Phil Healey, Rosalind Hudson, Paul McCaffrey, Chris Molan, Julian Mosedale, Kathryn Prewett, Andy Quelch, Mary-Claire Smith, Jennifer Ward.

Copyright permissions sought by Jackie Newman

Tel: 01865 888058 www.heinemann.co.uk

Introduction

Prometheus Unbound

He gave man speech, and speech created thought,
Which is the measure of the universe.

P. B. Shelley

AS YOU HAVE developed your skills in English you have become more aware of the power of words. You have seen how words can be used for many different purposes and have started to appreciate the influence they can have. You have learned how to read words with greater understanding. You have also learned how to use them with more effectiveness in your speech and writing.

Alongside this recognition of the power of words you need to be aware of the importance of thought. Skilled readers do not always believe everything they read. They question content and are aware of implications. They consider effects and find the words to express personal response. They listen to others with an awareness of the subtleties of tone and match this in their own speech. In writing they spend time gathering ideas and working out how they are going to get these across to their readers effectively. The brain is always active and lively, challenging new ideas, bringing personal experience to a text ... thinking.

The texts and activities in this book have been selected to help you develop your skills in English. As you work your way through the units be prepared to question and challenge the content. The answers are often not on the page but in your head, and the more thought you give to your work the better your progress will be.

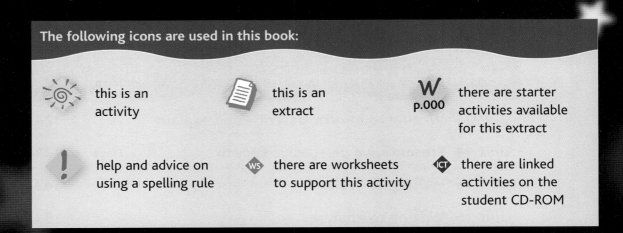

The following icons are used in this book:

this is an activity

this is an extract

p.000 there are starter activities available for this extract

help and advice on using a spelling rule

WS there are worksheets to support this activity

ICT there are linked activities on the student CD-ROM

CONTENTS

Section E – Speaking and listening   169

Section F – Words: spelling strategies and vocabulary   196

ACKNOWLEDGEMENTS

The Publishers gratefully acknowledge the following for permission to reproduce copyright material. Whilst every effort has been made to trace the copyright holders, in cases where this has proved unsuccessful or if any have inadvertently been overlooked, the Publishers will be pleased to make the necessary arrangements at the first opportunity.

Extract from list of 'knave insults' from *Shakespeare's Insults* by W. F. Hull and G. F. Ottchen published by Ebury, London, p.13. Extract from *Holes* by Louis Sachar published by Bloomsbury Children's Books 2000: reprinted by permission of Bloomsbury Publishing plc, p.16. Extract from *A Certain Age* by Rebecca Ray (Penguin Books 1998) Copyright © Rebecca Ray 1998: reprinted by permission of Penguin Books Limited, p.16. *The Breadwinner* by Leslie Howard Copyright © Leslie Howard, pp.19–21. 'Weep Not My Wanton' by A. E. Coppard, from *Dusky Ruth and Other Stories* published by Penguin Books: reprinted by permission of David Higham Associates Limited, pp.27–9. 'The Caged Bird in Springtime' by James Kirkup from *A Correct Compassion and Other Poems* published by Oxford University Press in 1954 and also in *Collected Shorter Poems Vol 1* published by Salzburg Press 1997 Copyright © James Kirkup: reprinted with the kind permission of the author, p.33. 'A Constable Calls' by Seamus Heaney from *New Selected Poems* published by Faber and Faber Limited: reprinted with permission of Faber and Faber Limited, p.35. 'Stereotype' by John Agard from *Mangoes and Bullets* published by Pluto Press 1985 Copyright © John Agard 1985: reprinted by kind permission of John Agard c/o Caroline Sheldon Literary Agency, p.39. 'Dress Sense' by David Kitchen Copyright © David Kitchen: reprinted with the kind permission of the author, p.45. 'Dread-lock style' by Lesley Miranda found in *Poetry Jump Up* published by Puffin, p.46. Extract from *Whispers in the Graveyard* by Theresa Breslin published by Mammoth Copyright © Theresa Breslin 1994: reprinted by permission of Laura Cecil Literary Agency on behalf of Theresa Breslin, p.48. Extract from *Throwaways* by Ian Strachan Copyright © Ian Strachan: reprinted by permission of Ian Strachan c/o Caroline Sheldon Literary Agency, p.49. Extract from 'Pawley's People' from *The Starlit Corridor* by John Wyndam: reprinted by permission of David Higham Associates Limited, p.49. Extract from *Kit's Wilderness* by David Almond published by Hodder 1999 © David Almond. Reproduced by permission of Hodder & Stoughton Limited, p.50. Extract from *The Giver* by Lowis Lowry, published by Collins 1999 Copyright © Lowis Lowry 1999: reprinted by permission of HarperCollins Publishers, p.50. Extract from *Postcard from No-Man's Land* by Aidan Chambers published by Bodley Head: used by permission of The Random House Group Limited, p.50. Extract from 'Monster in the Closet' by Jane Yole, first published in *Bruce Coville's Book of Monsters* published by Scholastic Inc Copyright © 1993 Jane Yolen: reprinted by permission of Curtis Brown Ltd, New York, p.51–3. Extracts from *Stone Cold* by Robert Swindells (Hamish Hamilton 1993) Copyright © Robert Swindells 1993: reprinted by permission of Penguin Books Limited, pp.56–8 and 184. Extract from the *Escape* section of the Observer, 12th August, 2001 (a piece on phrase books by Joanne O'Connor) Copyright © The Observer: used with permission, pp.61–2. Extract from *Neither Here Nor There* by Bill Bryson © Bill Bryson, published by Blackswan, a division of Transworld Publishers; all rights reserved: used by permission of the publishers, p.67. Excerpt from *Travels With Fortune: An African Adventure* by Christina Dodwell (London: W. H. Allen/Virgin Publishing 1979) Copyright © Christina Dodwell: reprinted with kind permission of the author, p.69. Extract from *Silent Spring* by Rachel Carson published by Hamish Hamilton: reprinted by permission of Laurence Pollinger Limited, pp.71-2. 'On Going to Meet a Zen Master in the Kyushu Mountains and Not Finding Him' by Don Paterson from *God's Gift to Women*, published by Faber and Faber Limited: reprinted by permission of Faber and Faber Limited, p.75. 'Poem Against Capital Punishment' by Roger McGough from *Defying Gravity* published by Penguin Books. Copyright © Roger McGough: reprinted by permission of Peters Fraser & Dunlop on behalf of Roger McGough, p.76. 'Yes' by Adrian Mitchell, from *Balloon Lagoon*, published by Orchard Books © Adrian Mitchell: reprinted by permission of Peters Fraser & Dunlop on behalf of Adrian Mitchell (Educational Health Warning: Adrian Mitchell asks that none of his poems are used in connection with any examination whatsoever), p.78. 'First Ice' by Andrei Voznesensky Copyright © Andrej Voznesensky: reprinted by permission of Russian Author's Society on behalf of Andrej Voznesensky, p.83. Cover of 'John Barnes' autobiography published by Hodder & Stoughton Limited (Photo © Jean-Francois Talivez): reprinted with the kind permission of Jean-Francois Talivez and Hodder & Stoughton Limited, p.85. Cover of *Long Walk to Freedom* Nelson Mandela published by Little Brown & Co, p.85. Extract from *Falling Leaves Return to Their Roots: The True Story of an Unwanted Chinese Daughter* by Adeline Yen Mah (Michael Joseph 1997) Copyright © Adeline Yen Mah 1997: reprinted by permission of Penguin Books Limited, p.86. Extract from *Is That It?* by Bob Geldoff, published by Macmillan Copyright © Bob Geldoff: reprinted by permission of Macmillan, pp.87 and 97. Extract from *All Points North* by Siman Armitage (Viking 1998) Copyright © Simon Armitage 1998: reprinted by permission of Penguin Books Limited, pp.90–1. Extract from *Oleander Jacaranda* by Penelope Lively published by Penguin Books: reprinted by permission of David Higham Associates Limited, pp.98–9. Extract from *Lark Rise to Candleford* by Flora Thompson (1945) published by Oxford University Press: reprinted by permission of Oxford University Press, p.94. 'Clear Complexion Advert' reprinted with the kind permission of Jessup Marketing, p.100. 'Opus – beyerdynamic Advert' reprinted with the kind permission of Beyerdynamic, p.104. Extract from 'Frog Tours leaflet' reprinted with the kind permission of Frog Tours, p.102. WDCS banner: reprinted with the kind permission of WDCS (Whale and Dolphin Conservation Society), p.102. Two adverts and an extract from the Barnardo's website: reprinted with the kind permission of Barnardo's, pp.107 and 109–10. 'Rumble in the Countryside' by Joanne Murphy, from 'The Stockport Express': reprinted with permission, p.117. Extract from *I Know Why The Caged Bird Sings* by Maya Angelou published by Virago Copyright © Maya Angelou: reprinted by permission of Time Warner Books UK, pp.120–1. Various extracts from *The Mysterious Case of the Mary Celeste* published by Tressell Publications 1981, pp.131–3. Extract from *Animal Farm* by George Orwell Copyright © George Orwell: reprinted by permission of Bill Hamilton as the Literary Executor of the Estate of the Late Sonia Brownell Orwell and Secker & Warburg Limited c/o A. M. Heath, pp.138–9 and 141–2. Extracts from *The Score: Facts about Drugs*: reproduced by permission of Health Promotion England, p.146. 'The Listeners' by Walter de la Mare, from *The Complete Poems of Walter de la Mare 1969*: reprinted by permission of The Literary Trustees of Walter de la Mare and the Society of Authors as their representative, p.164. Blue Cross logo and text: reprinted with the kind permission of the Blue Cross, p.166. Falklands Speech by Margaret Thatcher Copyright © 1997 published by HarperCollins Publishers: reproduced by permission of HarperCollins Publishers, p.173. Extract from *Blood Brothers* by Willy Russell published by Methuen: reprinted by permission of Methuen Publishing Limited, pp.178–81.

Section A ◆ Reading literature
Introduction

In this book the word 'literature' is used to describe the range of written material that is linked with the imagination and making things up. This includes prose, which may be short stories or novels, poetry or play scripts.

In Year 8 you will have developed your understanding of genre and your awareness and appreciation of writers' techniques. You will have explored literature from different cultures, and reflected on the main differences between standard English and dialect.

You will be building on these skills in the three units of work in this section.

In Unit 1, *Appreciating variety in language*, you will develop your understanding of how language is used and how it changes over time. You will think about the variety and richness of language and relate major writers to their historical context.

In Unit 2, *Reading in depth*, you will examine two texts closely. You will learn how to interpret detail appropriately and how to refer to the text when answering questions. You will identify the similarities and differences between the two texts, and develop your skills in writing about these.

In Unit 3, *Recognising the writer's stance*, you will consider how different writers present their ideas. You will compare the themes and styles of two poets, and will learn to distinguish between the attitudes of characters and those of the writer.

Unit 4 tests you on the skills you will develop as you work carefully through the three units.

This unit will help you to:
- ◆ understand that language changes over time
- ◆ develop your understanding of how language works
- ◆ relate major writers to their historical context
- ◆ recognise some features of highly regarded texts.

How English has changed

Do you recognise the language used in the extract below? Try reading it aloud. The ' þ' is called a thorn and is pronounced as 'th'.

The Battle of Maldon

p.199

Her lið ure ealdor eall forheapen,
ʒod on ʒreote. A mæʒ ʒnornian
se ðe nu fram þis piʒpleʒan pendan þenceð.
Ic eom frod feores. Fram ic ne pille,
5   ac ic me be healfe minum hlaforde,
be spa leofan men licʒan þence.

Old English poem

The language used in this extract is a very old form of English, which was once spoken and written. The extract is taken from a poem written to commemorate the Battle of Maldon, fought in AD 991. This type of English is called Old English, or Anglo-Saxon.

In AD 449, 542 years before this poem was written, Saxons, Angles and Jutes from powerful German nations had started to invade England. They brought their language with them and many words still used in English today are of German origin.

When trying to work out the meaning of Old English you should look for clues in the words:

Shares the same first three letters as 'here', or could mean 'she'.

Contains the word 'all'.

Does this remind you of 'in a heap'?

Her lið ure ealdor eall forheapen,

A bit like 'elder', a person of senior position.

This will help you to reach the line's actual meaning:
Here lies our chief all hewn down.

Activity 1 ᴵᶜᵀ

1 Re-read line 1 of the poem. Which two words can you match with these German words?

   a *hier* (German: here)   **b** *unser* (German: our)

2 By using what you know about word patterns, try to work out the Old English equivalent for these Modern English words:

   from   I   by   lord   this   years   of my   man

3 Check your guesses against this recent translation of these lines:

> Here lies our chief all hewn down,
> a noble man in the dust. He has cause ever to mourn
> who intends now to turn from this war-play.
> I am advanced in years. I will not hence,
> but I by the side of my lord,
> by so dear a man, intend to lie.

Middle English

The year 1066 marks the Battle of Hastings and the Norman invasion of England. The language introduced into Britain by the invader William the Conqueror was French. Over the centuries that followed this had an enormous impact on both spoken and written English. It has been estimated that some 10,000 French words came into English at that time. A few examples of these are:

| *place* | *appetite* | *calendar* | *prayer* | *honour* | *lieutenant* |

The language of this period is called Middle English. One of its most famous writers was Geoffrey Chaucer (1343–1400), whose best known work is *The Canterbury Tales*.

In this fictional work, a band of pilgrims (people who went on journeys to sacred places) meet at the Tabard Inn at Southwark, in London. They plan to travel to the shrine of St Thomas à Becket in Canterbury. They agree to liven up their journey by having a story-telling competition. Before each of the tales are told, Chaucer introduces the pilgrim telling that tale.

In the extract on page 10, we meet the Wife of Bath. You will probably recognise the language in the extract as English, but you may not understand it all. To help with understanding, the editors of Old and Middle English texts often include footnotes at the bottom of each page.

Activity 2

1 Here are the footnotes for the extract below, but the words and their meanings have been mixed up. As you read the extract for the first time, try to match the bold words to the correct meanings. The first one has been done for you.

Bathe	the church porch where a medieval marriage was made legal
scathe	a type of material
swich an haunt	a pity
Ypres and Gaunt	tightly fastened
the offrynge	at present, at the moment
wrooth	such a talent
coverchiefs	stockings
ground	now Bath, a town in the south of England
hosen	head-dresses
streite yteyd	French towns where the finest clothes were made
at chirche dore	the offerings made by the congregation to the priest (they would be made in order of rank)
as nowthe	annoyed

2 As you read the extract, try to find words influenced by these French words:
- *paroisse* (parish) ◆ *offrir* (offer) ◆ *charité* (charity) ◆ *compagnie* (company).

The wif of Bathe

p.199

A good WIF was ther of biside BATHE,
But she was somdel deef, and that was scathe.
Of clooth-makyng she hadde swich an haunt,
She passed hem of Ypres and of Gaunt.
5 In al the parisshe wif ne was ther noon
That to the offrynge bifore hire sholde goon;
And if ther dide, certeyn so wrooth was she,
That she was out of alle charitee.
Hir coverchiefs ful fyne weren of ground;
10 I dorste swere they weyeden ten pound
That on a Sonday weren upon hir heed.
Hir hosen weren of fyn scarlet reed,
Ful streite yteyd, and shoes ful moyste and newe.
Boold was hir face, and fair, and reed of hewe.
15 She was a worthy womman al hir lyve:
Housbondes at chirche dore she hadde fyve,
Withouten oother compaignye in youthe, –
But therof nedeth nat to speke as nowthe.

*from **The Canterbury Tales General Prologue** by Geoffrey Chaucer*

You might understand the passage about the Wife of Bath better if you change it into Modern English. Start by looking at each word on its own to get an idea of the meaning – for example:

Hir	hosen	weren	of	fyn	scarlet	reed (line 12)
Her	stockings	were	of	fine	scarlet	red

Ful	streite	yteyd,	and	shoes	ful	moyste	and	newe. (line 13)
Full	straight	tied,	and	shoes	full	moist	and	new.

It is not only the words that have changed over time but also the way we use them. Now that the words themselves have been rewritten in Modern English, your next step is to think about how complete sentences might be written. For example, we wouldn't write of fine *scarlet red*, *full straight tied* or *ful moyste* in Modern English. These are archaic forms. But we might write: *Her stockings were a lovely scarlet and tightly fastened, and her shoes were soft and new.*

Activity 3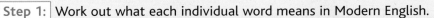

In pairs, rewrite in Modern English the passage about the Wife of Bath. This will help you to increase your understanding of how Modern English differs from Middle English. To do this activity you will need to work through the steps below. (Remember to use the footnotes to help you.)

Step 1: Work out what each individual word means in Modern English.

Step 2: Identify where the sentence structure or word order needs to be changed.

Step 3: Rewrite the whole passage as it might be written today.

Activity 4

One reason that Chaucer's work is still so popular is the detail he uses to describe his characters. Think about the Wife of Bath.

1 List in note form the different things you are told about her appearance.

2 What does her appearance suggest about the kind of woman she is?

3 Now think about the other things you are told about the Wife of Bath:

> In al the parisshe wif ne was ther noon
> That to the offrynge bifore hire sholde goon;
> And if ther dide, certeyn so wrooth was she,
> That she was out of alle charitee …
> Housbondes at chirche dore she hadde fyve,
> Withouten oother compaignye in youthe, –
> But therof nedeth nat to speke as nowthe.

What do these details tell you about the kind of woman she is? Does this extra information fit in with her appearance?

Early Modern English

1066 and the Battle of Hastings marked the start of the shift in the language from Old to Middle English. In 1476, William Caxton's printing press marked another significant change in the English language. The press provided more opportunities for people to write. With this came a need to develop a more standard form of English.

Written English in the period after the invention of the printing press was not so different from written English today. Most of the words used then can be found in a modern dictionary, but understanding them still requires some extra effort.

Probably the most famous writer of this Early Modern period is William Shakespeare (1564–1616). Shakespeare wrote many plays, including *Macbeth*. The central character, Macbeth, was once an honourable and brave soldier. However, ambition got the better of him. This led him to murder the King. He was also responsible for the deaths of many others. In the extract below, Macbeth realises that his life is not as it could have been.

There are a number of reasons why some of the words in this extract may be difficult for you to understand. These have been annotated.

Act 5 Scene 3

Sere means 'dried up' or 'withered'. You could guess at its meaning by looking at the phrase that follows it: 'the yellow leaf'.

> I have lived long enough. My way of life
> Is fall'n into the sere, the yellow leaf,
> And that which should accompany old age,
> As honour, love, obedience, troops of friends,
> I must not look to have; but in their stead,
> Curses, not loud but deep, mouth-honour, breath
> Which the poor heart would fain deny, and dare not.

*from **Macbeth** by William Shakespeare*

You may not have learned this word yet. The dictionary meaning of 'stead' is 'place'. So *in their stead* means 'in their place'. This may remind you of the word 'instead'.

This combination of words is rarely used now. *Mouth-honour* means 'flattery' or, literally, honour paid from the mouth.

When you come across words that you don't understand you can:

◆ use a dictionary
◆ try and work out what they suggest
◆ make a sensible guess based on what comes before or after them
◆ use your knowledge of other languages to help you – for example, can you find words in the *Macbeth* passage that come from the French words *accompagner* and *honneur*, and the German words *Freund* and *genug*?

Activity 5

In groups of three, carefully re-read the passage on page 12 from *Macbeth*. Use the methods listed after the extract to help you work out its meaning. Show your understanding of the passage by taking it in turns to explain:

- ◆ what Macbeth feels he should have at this time of life
- ◆ what he actually has
- ◆ how you think he feels about this.

The best and most obvious way to overcome unfamiliarity with Shakespeare's language is to find out more about it. One of the reasons he is still so popular is the variety and range of his words. Below are some examples of the insults he made up.
Try saying some of these insults aloud to a partner. Vary the tone of your voice to suit the insult. Where the words are unfamiliar, guess at their meanings. You could start your insult with *Thou art a ...* or *Thou art the ...* or *Get thee gone thou ...* .

Insults about knaves

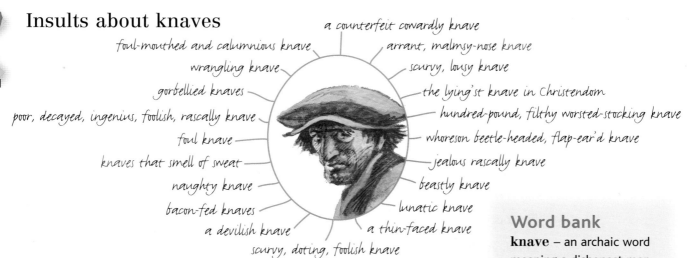

W p.201

Word bank
knave – an archaic word meaning a dishonest man

*from **Shakespeare's Insults** by W. F. Hull and G. F. Ottchen*

Activity 6

1 Examine the insults more closely to discover the range of Shakespeare's words. Group them under different headings – for example:

- ◆ insults about clothes
- ◆ insults about behaviour
- ◆ insults about looks.

Find as many different ways of grouping them as you can. Some insults may appear under more than one heading.

2 Now make up some original insults of your own to use against a celebrity you do not like. Use Modern English. Do not use commonly known insults or swear words. Aim, like Shakespeare, to use a wide range of words, and to make them as interesting and insulting as possible.

Modern English

By the nineteenth century, the English language was very close to what we might use today. But there were still some differences.

Read the extract below, which is from a novel by Charles Dickens (1812–1870). This extract is a long and complex sentence, packed with information about the setting. Sentences of this length appear less often in Modern English. The annotations show you some of the different parts of the sentence. Can you identify any others?

Prepositional phrase, combining the preposition 'in' and the noun phrases 'these times of ours'.

Subordinate clause, which gives extra information about the setting.

[In these times of ours,] [though concerning the exact year there is no need to be precise,] a boat of dirty and disreputable appearance, with two figures in it, floated on the Thames, between Southwark Bridge which is of iron, and London Bridge [which is of stone,] as an autumn evening was closing in.

Subordinate clause that links directly to the opening phrase and qualifies it.

Noun phrase, in which we are told more about the noun, a boat.

*from **Our Mutual Friend** by Charles DickensS*

Activity 7 ⬧ICT

Now read the next paragraph. The key details of the first two sentences have been underlined for you.

1 Pick out and write down the key details from the rest of the passage.

2 Check your key details with those of a partner. Discuss how you made your decisions about what to leave out.

3 Write a sentence advising another student on how to select key details.

On the look out

The figures in this boat were those of a strong man with ragged grizzled hair and a sun-browned face, and a dark girl of nineteen or twenty, sufficiently like him to be recognizable as his daughter. The girl rowed, pulling a pair of **sculls** very easily; the man, with **rudder-lines** slack in his hands,
5   and his hands loose in his waistband, kept an eager look out.
He had no net, hook, or line, and he could not be

a fisherman; his boat had no cushion for a sitter, no paint, no inscription, no appliance beyond a rusty boathook and a coil of rope, and he could not be a waterman; his boat was too crazy and too small to take in cargo for delivery, and

10 he could not be a lighterman or river-carrier; there was no clue to what he looked for, but he looked for something, with a most intent and searching gaze. The tide, which had turned an hour before, was running down, and his eyes watched every little race and eddy in its broad sweep, as the boat made slight head-way against it, or drove stern foremost before it, according as he directed

15 his daughter by a movement of his head.
She watched his face as **earnestly** as
he watched the river. But, in the
intensity of her look there was
a touch of dread or horror.

*from **Our Mutual Friend***
by Charles Dickens

Word bank
sculls – single oars
rudder-lines – ropes used to steer a boat
earnestly – seriously

Activity 8

Think about the details in the passage that help you to know it was not written in this century.

1 The man is described as having 'a sun-browned face' (line 2). What term is more commonly used today?

2 We are told that the man 'could not be a waterman'. 'Waterman' was a term used to describe a skilled boatman.

    a What other occupations are mentioned?   **b** What do you think they involved?
    c Why are these words unfamiliar today?

3 Find and list any other clues that suggest this text was written more than 100 years ago.

While Dickens's use of language may seem a little different at first, many features of his writing are found in modern stories – for example:

◆ his use of detail   ◆ the way he gets his readers' attention
◆ his methods of creating mystery and tension.

Activity 9 (WS)

Dickens's novels often have a dramatic opening. How does he create a sense of mystery and danger in the passage beginning on page 14? In your answer think about:

◆ the scene he sets
◆ the way he creates a sense of mystery around the man and the girl
◆ the way he makes us feel the man is searching for something dreadful.

British and American English

The English language is constantly changing. It is used in many places around the world and each place has developed its own vocabulary. So, for example, a text written in English by an American writer can often be distinguished from one written by an English writer.

Read the two extracts below. One has been written by an English writer, and one by an American.

'I was walking home and the sneakers fell from the sky,' he had told the judge. 'One hit me on the head.'

It had hurt too.

They hadn't exactly fallen from the sky. He had just walked out from a freeway overpass when the shoe hit him on the head.

Naturally he had no way of knowing they belonged to Clyde Livingston. In fact, the shoes were anything but sweet. Whoever had worn them had had a bad case of foot odor.

from **Holes** *by Louis Sachar*

Dad turned the corner when we got into town, right for the High Street, not left for the cafés. I didn't talk much, and Dad talked less, and I didn't say a thing when we turned the other way. I watched the wool shop go past, all the thirty-five-year-old mums who dress like they're sixty, and I wondered if knitting did that to you. They had a special sale on, with a basket out the front full of yellow balls for only 50p. I thought there'd be a lot of kids going round with yellow jumpers, come this Christmas.

from **A Certain Age** *by Rebecca Ray*

Activity 10 ⓦⓢ ⓘⓒⓣ

1 Can you identify the passage by the American writer and the one by the English writer? Talk about what helped you to identify the origins of the writers.

2 Make a chart like the one below. Then sort the words at the end of this page into pairs of American and English words with the same meaning.
Make a note of how you worked out the meaning of the American word.
Was it through:

- ◆ clues in the words themselves?
- ◆ television?
- ◆ your knowledge of word families?
- ◆ guesswork?

British English	American English	How I knew
autumn	fall	from TV

autumn semester cookie term recess nappy garbage break vacation fall holiday French-fries freeway chips rubbish biscuit diaper eraser allowance trainers rubber pavement motorway petrol pants sneakers sidewalk pocket-money drugstore gasoline chemist's trousers

English and the computer age

The arrival of the computer age has brought about one of the most rapid changes in the English language.

A new form of the language has grown up with the popularity of electronic messaging.

Electronic messages (e-messages) and electronic mail (e-mail) are ways of communicating online.

◆ In the former, both the sender and the receiver are logged on to their computers at the same time.

◆ In the latter, a message is left in a 'mail box' for later reading.

E-messages and e-mails are more like spoken English than written letters. As a result, different rules and expectations are developing around them.

Activity 11

Read the following e-mail messages between two friends.

1 In pairs, list any points you can make about:

◆ the punctuation

◆ greetings and farewells

◆ abbreviations

◆ style and tone

◆ letter cases (capitals and small letters)

◆ the correction of mistakes.

2 Now that you have studied the features of these e-mails, produce between five and ten short, clear instructions on how informal e-mails might be written.

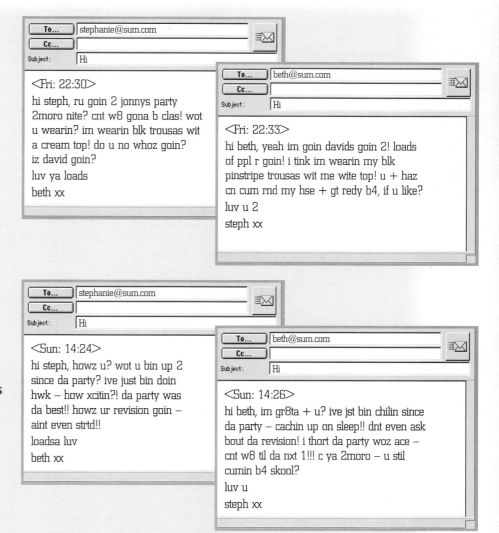

To... stephanie@sum.com
Cc...
Subject: Hi

<Fri: 22:30>
hi steph, ru goin 2 jonnys party 2moro nite? cnt w8 gona b clas! wot u wearin? im wearin blk trousas wit a cream top! do u no whoz goin? iz david goin?
luv ya loads
beth xx

To... beth@sum.com
Cc...
Subject: Hi

<Fri: 22:33>
hi beth, yeah im goin davids goin 2! loads of ppl r goin! i tink im wearin my blk pinstripe trousas wit me wite top! u + haz cn cum rnd my hse + gt redy b4, if u like?
luv u 2
steph xx

To... stephanie@sum.com
Cc...
Subject: Hi

<Sun: 14:24>
hi steph, howz u? wot u bin up 2 since da party? ive just bin doin hwk – how xcitin?! da party was da best!! howz ur revision goin – aint even strtd!!
loadsa luv
beth xx

To... beth@sum.com
Cc...
Subject: Hi

<Sun: 14:26>
hi beth, im gr8ta + u? ive jst bin chilin since da party – cachin up on sleep!! dnt even ask bout da revision! i thort da party woz ace – cnt w8 til da nxt 1!!! c ya 2moro – u stil cumin b4 skool?
luv u
steph xx

English across time

Activity 12

Below is a timeline, representing the history of the British Isles from 500AD to the present day. Look back through this unit to help you decide where the different events, labelled a–j below, should be placed along the timeline. Copy the timeline and indicate the date of the event and its appropriate position on the line.

a Invention of e-mail.

b More than 10,000 French words came into the English language.

c The English lost the Battle of Hastings to the Normans.

d William Shakespeare, possibly the most famous playwright of all times, wrote in Early Modern English: 'arrant, malmsy-nose knave'.

e Charles Dickens, author of *Our Mutual Friend*, wrote in Modern English: 'there was no clue to what he looked for, but he looked for something with intent and searching gaze'.

f The Battle of Maldon between the English and the Vikings gave rise to a poem, written in Old English.

g Invention of the first computer.

h William Caxton set up his printing press.

i The Saxons, the Angles and the Jutes, all from the most powerful German nations, start to invade Britain.

j Geoffrey Chaucer, author of *The Canterbury Tales*, wrote in Middle English: 'Husbondes at chirche dore she hadde fyve'.

|AD 500|AD 1000|AD 1500|AD 2000|

This unit will help you to:
- interpret detail
- use reference and quotation effectively
- develop your personal response
- compare texts by identifying similarities and differences
- evaluate your own writing about texts.

Interpreting detail

Sometimes in exams you are asked to read a text before you answer questions on it. Where this happens you need to apply the reading strategies you have been developing throughout Key Stage 3. Read the following short story closely and think about the detail you are given.

The Breadwinner

p.207

The parents of a boy of fourteen were waiting for him to come home with his first week's wages.

The mother had laid the table and was cutting some slices of bread and butter for tea. She was a little woman with a pinched face and a **spare** body, dressed in a blue
5 blouse and skirt, the front of the skirt covered with a starched white apron. She looked tired and frequently sighed heavily.

The father, sprawling inelegantly in an old armchair by the fireside, legs outstretched, was little too. He had watery blue eyes and a heavy brown moustache, which he sucked occasionally.

10 These people were plainly poor, for the room, though clean, was **meanly** furnished, and the thick pieces of bread and butter were the only food on the table.

As she prepared the meal, the woman from time to time looked contemptuously at her husband. He ignored her, raising his eyebrows, humming, or tapping his teeth now and then with his finger-nails, making a
15 pretence of being profoundly bored.

'You'll keep your hands off the money,' said the woman, obviously repeating something that she had already said several times before. 'I know what'll happen to it if you get hold of it. He'll give it to me. It'll pay the rent and buy us a bit of food, and not go into the till at the nearest public-house.'

20 'You shut your mouth,' said the man, quietly.

'I'll not shut my mouth!' cried the woman, in a quick burst of anger. 'Why should I shut my mouth? You've been boss here for long enough. I put up with it when you were bringing money into the house, but I'll not put up with it now. You're nobody here. Understand? *Nobody. I'm* boss and he'll hand the money to me!'

25 'We'll see about that,' said the man, leisurely poking the fire.

Nothing more was said for about five minutes.

Then the boy came in. He did not look older than ten or eleven years. He looked absurd in long trousers. The whites of his eyes against his black face gave him a startled expression.

30 The father got to his feet.

'Where's the money?' he demanded.

The boy looked from one to the other. He was afraid of his father. He licked his pale lips.

'Come on now,' said the man. 'Where's the money?'

35 'Don't give it to him,' said the woman. 'Don't give it to him, Billy. Give it to me.'

The father advanced on the boy, his teeth showing in a snarl under his big moustache.

'Where's the money?' he almost whispered.

The boy looked him straight in the eyes.

40 'I lost it,' he said.

'You – *what*?' cried his father.

'I lost it,' the boy repeated.

The man began to shout and wave his hands about.

'Lost it! *Lost* it! What are you talking about? How could you lose it?'

45 'It was in a packet,' said the boy, 'a little envelope. I lost it.'

'Where did you lose it?'

'I don't know. I must have dropped it in the street.'

'Did you go back and look for it?'

The boy nodded. 'I couldn't find it,' he said.

50 The man made a noise in his throat, half grunt, half moan – the sort of noise that an animal would make.

'So you lost it, did you?' he said. He stepped back a couple of paces and took off his belt – a wide, thick belt with a heavy brass buckle. 'Come here,' he said.

The boy, biting his lower lip so as to keep back the tears, advanced, and the man
55 raised his arm. The woman, motionless until that moment, leapt forward and seized it. Her husband, finding strength in his blind rage, pushed her aside easily. He brought the belt down on the boy's back. He beat him unmercifully about the body and legs. The boy sank to the floor, but did not cry out.

When the man had spent himself, he put on the belt and pulled the boy to his feet.

60 'Now you'll get off to bed,' he said.

'The lad wants some food,' said the woman.

'He'll go to bed. Go and wash yourself.'

Without a word the boy went into the **scullery** and washed his hands and face. When he had done this he went straight upstairs.

65 The man sat down at the table, ate some bread and butter and drank two cups of tea. The woman ate nothing. She sat opposite him, never taking her eyes from his face, looking with hatred at him. Just as before, he took no notice of her, ignored her, behaved as if she were not there at all.

When he had finished the meal he went out.

70 Immediately he had shut the door the woman jumped to her feet and ran upstairs to the boy's room.

He was sobbing bitterly, his face buried in the pillow. She sat on the edge of the bed and put her arms about him, pressed him close to her breast, ran her fingers through his disordered hair, whispered **endearments**, consoling him. He let her do

75 this, finding comfort in her caresses, relief in his own tears.

After a while his weeping ceased. He raised his head and smiled at her, his wet eyes bright. Then he put his hand under the pillow and withdrew a small dirty envelope.

'Here's the money,' he whispered.

She took the envelope and opened it and pulled

80 out a long strip of paper with some figures on it – a **ten shilling note** and a **sixpence**.

The Breadwinner by Leslie Harward

> ### Word bank
> **spare** – thin or lean
> **meanly** – poorly, not generously
> **scullery** – back kitchen
> **endearments** – words of affection
> **ten shilling note** – old money: 50 pence
> **sixpence** – old money: 2 ½ pence

When answering questions on a text, you need to:

◆ find the relevant detail in the text ◆ interpret and comment on this detail.

The demonstration on page 22 will show you how to do this.

Think about this question:

> *What impressions are you given of the mother from lines 1 to 6 ('The parents' ... to '... sighed heavily.')?*

Step 1: The first thing you should do is to re-read lines 1 to 6. This is where you are given information about the mother. Highlight or take note of details that seem particularly significant:

> *She was a little woman with <u>a pinched face and a spare body</u>, dressed in a blue blouse and skirt, the front of the skirt covered with <u>a starched white apron. She looked tired and frequently sighed heavily</u>.*

Step 2: Now ask yourself questions like the ones below.

◆ Why has the writer used particular words like 'pinched' and 'sighed'?

◆ What is the significance of the starched white apron?

◆ What is the writer trying to tell the reader about the mother?

Match the details to what they suggest.

a pinched face and a spare body   she was unhappy

a starched white apron   she kept herself clean and tidy

she frequently sighed heavily   she was unwell and/or underfed

Step 3: Finally, you need to answer the question 'What impressions are you given of the mother from lines 1 to 6?' by putting the details together with what they tell you. The following answer is annotated to show you the student's thoughts as he wrote.

I write in standard English, as this is the appropriate form for written answers.

The story tells me she is 'little'. I have used my own word 'small' for my explanation.

I know 'starched' means it's been made as crease-free as possible.

Instead of saying 'it suggests' again, for variety I use the phrase 'which implies that'.

The mother was a small woman. She might not have been very well [as she is described as] having 'a pinched face and a spare body'. She wore a starched white apron over the front of her skirt. As the apron was starched it suggests she took care to stay clean and tidy. She looked tired and sighed heavily, [which implies that] she was unhappy or that something was worrying her.

I cannot be sure about this. Therefore, I say 'might'. Because I'm not sure, I introduce evidence to back up my point. I use the words 'as she is described as' to introduce my evidence.

For variety, I give my evidence first in this sentence. I introduce the evidence with the word 'as' and I follow it with 'it suggests' to introduce my thoughts about what 'starched' tells me.

Activity 1

Re-read lines 12 to 26 of the passage from *The Breadwinner* (from 'As she prepared ...' to '... for about five minutes.'). Use the three steps on page 22 to help you answer this question:

> *What do you learn about the relationship between the father and the mother?*

Write about the details you are given in the passage and what these details tell you.

Using references and quotations

When you are answering questions about a text it is important to refer to details in it to support the comments you make. You can do the following.

◆ Refer to a particular detail in the text.

Comment	Evidence
It sounds as though the father drinks a lot.	The mother wants the money to buy food and pay the rent, and she is afraid that if the father gets it he will spend it on drink.

◆ Use a quotation.

Comment	Evidence
It sounds as though the father drinks a lot.	The mother wants the money to buy food and pay the rent, and she is afraid that if the father gets it, it will 'go into the till at the nearest public-house'.

Notice that quotation marks are placed around the words taken from the text.

Activity 2

Find a relevant detail or quotation to support the following comments about the boy, then use it within a sentence. The first one has been done for you.

Comment	Evidence
The boy looked younger than his age.	We are told that the boy was fourteen but that 'He did not look older than ten or eleven years'.
The boy shows courage when dealing with his father.	
The boy refuses to give in to his father.	
The boy is very upset by what has happened.	
The boy cares about his mother.	

Developing a personal response

In *The Breadwinner* the writer presents the reader with a story. This story will affect different readers in different ways, depending on their backgrounds, feelings and life experiences. You need to be able to work out how you are affected by it and why. This area of response to literature is often called personal response.

Look at the question below, which targets a personal response.

> *What do you think of the way the father behaves in this story?*

This question is about two things:

◆ the father's behaviour   ◆ your thoughts on this.

In order to answer this you need first to consider the questions listed in Activity 3.

Activity 3

Discuss the following questions with a partner and make brief notes on your answers.

1 How does the father behave towards his wife and his son? Look at the text for evidence.

2 Why does he behave in this way? Can you find any clues in the text? You may need to read between the lines (in other words, the clues may not be obvious).

3 Have you come across anyone like the father? Think about people you know personally and also characters on television or in books.

4 What do you think about his actions?

5 How do his actions make you feel? Why do they make you feel like this?

6 Review what you have discussed. Do you and your partner have different opinions on any of the questions? What are the reasons for the difference?

Activity 4

1 Now use your notes from Activity 3 to help you answer the question:

> *What do you think of the way the father behaves in* The Breadwinner?

It may help you to organise your answer in this way.

Paragraph 1 Describe how the father behaves towards the mother. Comment on his behaviour and use evidence from the text to support your points.

Paragraph 2 Describe how the father behaves towards his son. Comment on his behaviour and use evidence from the text to support your points.

Paragraph 3 Explain how you think and feel about the father's behaviour. Give reasons for your thoughts and feelings.

Remember to write in a formal style. You could also use the following words and phrases in your answer:

- *as, so, because*
- *this would imply that*
- *gives an impression of*
- *it would seem that*
- *implying that, possibly*
- *however, this could mean that*
- *this suggests that*
- *causing me to think that*

2 When you have completed your answer, check that you have developed your ideas and referred to the text by:

- numbering the different points you have made (if you have made the same point twice you need to delete one of them)
- underlining all references to the text (if you have made a point without giving evidence, you need to insert the evidence).

Always check your answers carefully in an exam.
You can cross out and add details. This shows the
examiner that you are thinking carefully about the question.

Comparing texts

Students are often asked to compare texts in an exam. When you compare two things you are looking for the similarities and differences between them. In order to identify these it is helpful to make notes.

Activity 5 WS ICT

Make a copy of the chart below. The first column gives you the subject to consider. Complete the second column by making notes on *The Breadwinner*. Remember that for notes you:

- *do* use abbreviated forms of words
- *do not* write in sentences.

Subject	The Breadwinner	Weep Not My Wanton
Setting		
Appearance of the father		
Appearance of the mother		
What the boy is like		
How the father speaks		
How the father acts		
Reasons for the physical violence		
Actions of the mother		

Now read the following short story and complete the third column of your chart. Highlight any points of similarity or difference.

Weep Not My Wanton

Air and light on Sack Down at summer sunset were soft as ointment and sweet as milk. The **toilers** had mostly given over; their ploughs and **harrows** were left to the abandoned fields; they had taken their wages and gone, or were going, home; but at the crown of the hill a black barn stood by the roadside, and in
5 its yard, amid sounds of anguish, a score of young boar pigs were being **gelded** by two brown lads and a gipsy fellow. If a man desired peace he would step fast down the hill towards Arwall with finger in ear until he came to quiet at a bank overlooking slopes of barley.

Four figures, a labourer and his family, travelled slowly up the road
10 proceeding across the hill, a sound mingling dully with their steps – the voice of the man.

'You're a naughty, naughty – you're a vurry, *vurry* naughty boy! Oi can't think what's comen tyeh!'

The father towered above the tiny figure shuffling under his elbow, and
15 kept his eyes stupidly fixed upon him. He saw a thin boy, a spare boy, a very shrunken boy of seven or eight years, crying quietly. He let no grief out of his lip, but his white face was streaming with dirty tears. He wore a man's cap, an unclean sailor jacket, large **knickerbockers** that made a mockery of his lean joints, a pair of women's button
20 boots, and he looked straight ahead.

'The idear! To go and lose a sixpence like that then! Where d'ye think yer'll land yerself, ay? Wher'd I be if I kept on losing sixpences, ay? A creature like you, ay!' and lifting his heavy hand the man struck the boy a blow behind with shock enough to disturb a heifer. They went on, the child with sobs that you
25 could feel rather than hear. As they passed the black barn the gipsy bawled encouragingly: 'Selp me, father, that's a good 'un, wallop his trousers!'

But the man ignored him, as he ignored the yell of the pig and the voice of the lark rioting above them all; he continued his **litany**:

'You're a naughty, naughty *boy*, an' I dunno what's comen tyeh!'
30 The woman, a poor slip of a woman she was, walked behind them with a smaller child: she seemed to have no desire to shield the boy or to placate the man. She did not seem to notice them, and led the toddling babe, to whom she gabbled, some paces to the rear of the man of anger. He was a great figure with a bronzed face; his trousers were tied at the knee, his wicker bag was
35 slung over his shoulder. With his free and massive hand he held the hand of the boy. He was slightly drunk, and walked with his legs somewhat wide, at the beginning of each stride lifting his heel higher than was required, and at the end of it placing his foot firmly but **obliquely** inwards. There were two bright medals on the breast of his waistcoat, presumably for valour; he was perhaps
40 a man who would stand upon his rights and his dignities, such as they were – but then he was drunk. He only ceased his complaining to gaze swayingly at the boy; then he struck him. The boy, crying quietly, made no effort to avoid or resist him.

'You understand me, you bad boy! As long as you're with me you got to
45 come under collar. And wher'll you be next I *dunno*, a bad creature like you, ay! An' then to turn roun' an' answer me! *I dunno*! I dunno *what's* comen tyeh. Ye know ye lost that sixpence through **glammering** about. Wher d'ye lose it, ay? Wher d'ye lose it, ay?'

At these questions he seized the boy by the neck and shook
50 him as a child does a bottle of water. The baby behind them was taken with little gusts of laughter at the sight, and the woman cooed back playfully at her.

'George, George!' yelled the woman.

The man turned round.
55 'Look after Annie!' she yelled again.

'What's up?' he called.

Her only answer was a giggle of laughter as she disappeared behind a hedge. The child toddled up to its father and took his
60 hand, while the quiet boy took her other hand with relief. She laughed up into their faces, and the man resumed his **homily**.

'He's a bad, bad boy.
65 He's a vurry *naughty* bad boy!'

By and by the woman came shuffling after them; the boy looked furtively around and dropped his sister's hand.

'Carm on, me beauty!' cried the man, lifting the girl to his shoulder. 'He's a bad boy; you 'ave a ride on your daddy.'

70 They went on alone and the woman joined the boy. He looked up at her with a sad face.

'O, my Christ, Johnny!' she said, putting her arms round the boy, 'what's 'e bin doin' to yeh? Yer face is all blood!'

'It's only me nose, mother. Here,' he whispered, 'here's the tanner.'

75 They went together down the hill towards the inn, which had already a light in its windows. The screams from the barn had ceased, and a cart passed them full of young pigs, bloody and subdued. The hill began to resume its old **dominion** of soft sounds. It was nearly nine o'clock, and one anxious farmer still made hay although, on this side of the down, day had declined, and with a greyness that came not from 80 the sky, but crept up from the world.

*adapted from **Weep Not My Wanton** by A. E. Coppard*

Word bank

toilers – workers
harrows – hand-held plough
gelded – castrated
knickerbockers – loose breeches gathered at the knee
litany – a long list (of the boy's wrongdoings)
obliquely – at a slant
glammering – dialect word for play-acting
homily – lecture or sermon
dominion – influence or control

You have identified some of the similarities and differences between *The Breadwinner* and *Weep Not My Wanton*. Now look more closely at the mothers in each of these passages.

The mother in *The Breadwinner*
She was a little woman with a pinched face and a spare body, dressed in a blue blouse and skirt, the front of the skirt covered with a starched white apron. She looked tired and frequently sighed heavily.

Thinks husband will spend money on drink.
Looks 'contemptuously at her husband'.
Stands up to husband – 'I'll not shut my mouth!'
Has son of fourteen.
Tries to defend son – seizes her husband's arm.
Looks with hatred at husband.
Is very close to son – physically comforts him.
Prepared to let son suffer to get money.

The mother in *Weep Not My Wanton*
... a poor slip of a woman ...

Walks behind husband.
Seems 'to have no desire to shield the boy'.
Has son of seven or eight and a toddler.
Husband is drunk.
Doesn't confront husband – does distract him with 'a giggle of laughter'.
Distressed by what happens – physically comforts boy.
Seems to know boy kept money for her.

Activity 6

Think about the information given about the mothers in *The Breadwinner* and *Weep Not My Wanton*. In pairs or small groups discuss the following question and bullet points. Take notes on any areas where there are differences of views and the reasons for these.

Which mother do you feel most sympathy with?

Talk about:

◆ how each mother deals with her husband
◆ how each mother deals with her son
◆ whether each mother was right to act as she did
◆ other actions each mother could have taken.

Activity 7 ◀ICT▶

Now you are ready to put all the pieces together. You have 40 minutes to write your answer to the following:

> *Compare the mother in* The Breadwinner *with the mother in* Weep Not My Wanton, *and explain your thoughts and feelings about them.*

It may help you to organise your answer in this way:

Step 1: Write about the mother in *The Breadwinner*.

Step 2: Write about the mother in *Weep Not My Wanton*.

Step 3: Point out the similarities and differences between them.

Step 4: Explain your thoughts and feelings about both mothers.

Remember to:

◆ select appropriate detail
◆ refer to the text and use quotations
◆ make clear points of similarity and difference
◆ develop your own point of view.

Your writing should:

◆ be in standard English
◆ be mainly in the present tense
◆ link ideas fluently.

Below are some useful sentence and paragraph starters.

In contrast to …	However …
Nevertheless …	Whereas …
Similarly …	In both cases …
They are similar (different) in so far as …	Both women …

When you have completed your writing, assess it by highlighting or annotating:

◆ points of similarity and difference
◆ references and quotations
◆ areas where you have developed a personal viewpoint.

Award your work a mark from 1 to 10. Give three clear reasons for the mark you have awarded. State one area where your work could be improved.

This unit will help you to:

◆ **identify the writer's voice**

◆ **recognise layers of meaning**

◆ **consider the impact of the cultural context**

◆ **compare the themes and styles of two poets**

◆ **distinguish between the attitudes of characters and those of the writer.**

Identifying the voice

How much do you learn about a writer from his or her writing? Talk about the following statements. Do you agree with them? Do they apply to different things you have read?

> He said it, so he must believe it.

> A writer's work often reveals his or her cultural background.

> Writers sometimes use characters to make their points for them.

> A writer sometimes disagrees with his characters – that's the whole point!

> A writer creates a world – he doesn't have to believe in it.

> Just because it's written down doesn't mean it's true.

> You can tell it's not an English writer because of the way it's written.

> Writers don't always say what they mean or mean what they say.

> If a writer uses the first person, then he or she is speaking directly to the reader.

As you may have concluded, a writer will not always speak directly to the reader, even when s/he uses the first person. 'The Caged Bird in Springtime' is an example of this.

Activity 1

As you read the following poem:

◆ list the clues you are given to help you identify the owner of the voice

◆ note the point at which you identify with certainty the owner of the voice.

The Caged Bird in Springtime

What can it be,
This curious anxiety?
It is as if I wanted
To fly away from here.

5 But how absurd!
I have never flown in my life,
And I do not know
What flying means, though I have heard,
Of course, something about it.

10 Why do I peck the wires of this little cage?
It is the only nest I have ever known.
But I want to build my own,
High in the secret branches of the air.

I cannot quite remember how
15 It is done, but I know
That what I want to do
Cannot be done here.

I have all I need –
Seed and water, air and light.
20 Why, then, do I weep with anguish,
And beat my head and my wings
Against those sharp wires, while the children
Smile at each other, saying 'Hark how he sings?'

James Kirkup

Activity 2 (WS) (ICT)

1 From the poem, identify the following.
    ◆ What the bird's life is like.   ◆ What the bird feels that it wants to do.

2 Words like 'curious anxiety' (line 2) show the reader directly how the bird feels. Other words such as 'little cage' (line 10) show indirectly how the bird feels. Think about the difference between these before identifying more examples of words being used to show the bird's feelings:
    ◆ directly   ◆ indirectly.

3 What misunderstanding is shown in the last line of the poem? What is the significance of this?

4 In no more than 100 words for each, summarise the point of view expressed in the poem by:
    ◆ the bird   ◆ the writer.

Analysing a poem

As we analyse a poem we often find that it can be interpreted in more than one way. Use 'The Caged Bird in Springtime' as an example.

- ◆ Does it have to be about a bird?
- ◆ Is there any way it could be about a person?
- ◆ Could it be about a teacher or a parent, for example?
- ◆ Could it be about someone who lives in a city or in the countryside?
- ◆ Could it be about someone like you?

Activity 3

1 Choose a person you think 'The Caged Bird in Springtime' could be about. Re-read the poem with a partner and talk about what each line means for that person.

2 Why do you think the writer uses the voice of a bird in this poem? Give at least two reasons.

Looking for clues

At times the writer seems to speak directly to the reader drawing on personal experience. The reader can sometimes tell when this is happening because there are clues in the text.

Activity 4 (ws)

1 Read 'A Constable Calls' closely several times. It tells of a visit by a constable (policeman). To help you decide if it is based on a memory of something that happened to the poet, make a chart like the one below and fill in the 'Details' column.

The memory	Details relating to the memory
The policeman's bicycle	
The policeman – clothing – physical appearance – items he carries	
The policeman's actions	
The father's actions/words	
The son's feelings	

If you have a photocopy of the poem you could highlight and annotate these things.

2 Giving reasons based on your notes, talk with a partner about whether you think the writer of the poem is speaking directly to the reader.

A Constable Calls

His bicycle stood at the window-sill,
The rubber cowl of a mud-splasher
Skirting the front mudguard,
Its fat black handlegrips

5 Heating in sunlight, the 'spud'
Of the dynamo gleaming and cocked back,
The pedal treads hanging relieved
Of the boot of the law.

His cap was upside down
10 On the floor, next his chair.
The line of its pressure ran like a **bevel**
In his slightly sweating hair.

He had unstrapped
The heavy **ledger**, and my father
15 Was making **tillage** returns
In **acres, roods, and perches**.

Arithmetic and fear.
I sat staring at the polished holster
With its buttoned flap, the braid cord
20 Looped into the revolver butt.

'Any other root crops?
Mangolds? Marrowstems? Anything like that?'
'No.' But was there not a line
Of turnips where the seed ran out
25 In the potato field? I assumed
Small guilts and sat
Imagining the black hole in the barracks.
He stood up, shifted the **baton-case**

Further round on his belt,
30 Closed **the domesday book**,
Fitted his cap back with two hands,
And looked at me as he said goodbye.

A shadow bobbed in the window.
He was snapping the carrier spring
35 Over the ledger. His boot pushed off
And the bicycle ticked, ticked, ticked.

Seamus Heaney

Word bank

bevel – sloping edge
ledger – account book
tillage – produce of
the land
acres, roods, and
perches – different
measurements of area
and length
baton-case – truncheon
case
the domesday book –
the original Domesday or
Doomsday Book was a
survey of the land of
England in 1086

Thinking about the cultural context

Sometimes it helps our understanding of a poem to have some awareness of the cultural context in which it was written. Seamus Heaney, who wrote 'A Constable Calls', is an Irish poet. He was raised as a Roman Catholic. He lived on his father's small farm in Northern Ireland, where there was conflict and suspicion between the Roman Catholic and Protestant communities. The constable in the poem would have been a Protestant.

Activity 5 WS ICT

Re-read 'A Constable Calls' (page 35) closely. How does the additional information about the cultural context help you to a better understanding of:

- the way Heaney describes the bicycle – for example, 'Its fat black handlegrips' (line 4)?
- the way Heaney describes the constable – for example, 'the boot of the law' (line 8)?
- Heaney's fascination with the gun?
- the father's single-word reply (line 23)?
- Heaney's feelings of guilt?
- the final line of the poem?

If you are working on a photocopy of the poem you could add to your annotations.

Looking at features of style

One of the most distinctive qualities of Heaney's poetry is the way he uses the sounds of words to create particular effects. Below are some features of 'A Constable Calls' which outline the poet's use of pauses, rhyme and sound.

Pauses
When a line of poetry has a strong pause at the end it is called 'end-stopped'. For example:
His bicycle stood at the window-sill,
When a line of poetry moves on to the next line with almost no pause it is called 'run-on'. For example:
The rubber cowl of a mud-splasher *Skirting the front mudguard,*
The effect of this continuity is called 'enjambment'.

Rhyme

End rhyme, where rhyme occurs at the close of lines, only appears once in this poem with 'chair' and 'hair' in the third stanza. However, Heaney does use internal rhyme and half-rhyme. For example:

And looked at me as he said goodbye (internal rhyme).

On the floor, next his chair (internal half-rhyme).

This has the effect of binding words together within a line or of making connections between lines.

Sound

Repetitions of sound are used to produce echoes within and between lines. Where there is repetition of consonant sounds, it is called consonance. Below, the repetition of the 'b' and 'ck' sounds reinforces a sense of the harshness of the imagined place.

… the black hole in the barracks.

Where there is repetition of vowel sounds, it is called assonance. For example:

Its fat black handlegrips

Here the repetition of the 'a' sound links the three words and emphasises the starkness of the description.

Activity 6

(WS)

1 Heaney uses a variety of end-stopped and run-on lines, including ones between stanzas. This directly affects the way the poem is read aloud. In pairs, re-read 'A Constable Calls' aloud, taking particular notice of punctuation.

2 Find and copy (or highlight and annotate) at least two other examples of internal rhyme or half-rhyme. Try to explain why Heaney has used rhyme in this way.

3 Copy (or highlight and annotate) as many other examples of both consonance and assonance as you can find. Try to explain why Heaney has used sound in this way. What is it about the words that he wants the reader to notice and perhaps remember?

Exploring attitudes and issues

The poet John Agard was born in Guyana, on the north-east coast of South America, when it was still a British colony. He moved to England in 1977 when he was 28 years old. He continues to live, write and perform his poetry there. The West Indian culture has a significant influence on what he writes and how he writes. In his poem, which appears opposite, he explores the concept of the West Indian stereotype.

Activity 7

Before reading John Agard's poem 'Stereotype', work in pairs to do the following:

1 Chart what you already know about West Indian culture. It might help you to think about:

- ◆ place names
- ◆ types of foods
- ◆ carnivals
- ◆ traditions
- ◆ famous people
- ◆ religion
- ◆ types of music.

2 Discuss what is meant by the term 'stereotype'. It might help you to think about:

- ◆ different types of stereotypes
- ◆ how you stereotype people from different countries.

Now read the poem.

Stereotype

I'm a fullblooded
West Indian stereotype
See me straw hat?
Watch it good

5 I'm a fullblooded
West Indian stereotype
You ask
if I got riddum
in me blood

10 You going ask!
Man just beat de drum
and don't forget
to pour de rum

I'm a fullblooded
15 West Indian stereotype
You say
I suppose you can show
us the **limbo**, can't you?
How you know!

20 How you know!
You sure
you don't want me
sing you a **calypso** too
How about that

25 I'm a fullblooded
West Indian stereotype
You call me
happy-go-lucky
Yes that's me

30 dressing fancy
and chasing woman
if you think ah lie
bring yuh sister

I'm a fullblooded
35 West Indian stereotype
You wonder
where do you people
get such riddum
could it be the sunshine

40 My goodness
just listen to that steelband

Isn't there one thing
you forgot to ask
go on man ask ask

45 This native will answer anything
How about cricket?
I suppose you're good at it?
Hear this man
good at it!

50 Put de **willow**
in me hand
and watch me strike
de **boundary**

Yes I'm a fullblooded
55 West Indian stereotype

that's why I
graduated from Oxford University
with a degree
in **anthropology**

John Agard

Word bank

limbo – where the dancer literally bends over backwards to pass under a bar

calypso – a West Indian song that has a topical meaning

willow – another way of saying 'cricket bat'

boundary – the edge of the field on which cricket is played

anthropology – the study of other people and their customs

Activity 8 (WS)

Agard's poetry is often performed. The sounds of the words are very important, as is the way the words are spoken.

1 In pairs, prepare a reading of the poem. The first part of your preparation is to analyse the way Agard uses language to create certain effects. You can do this by asking a series of questions. Study this analysis of the first two stanzas of the poem closely.

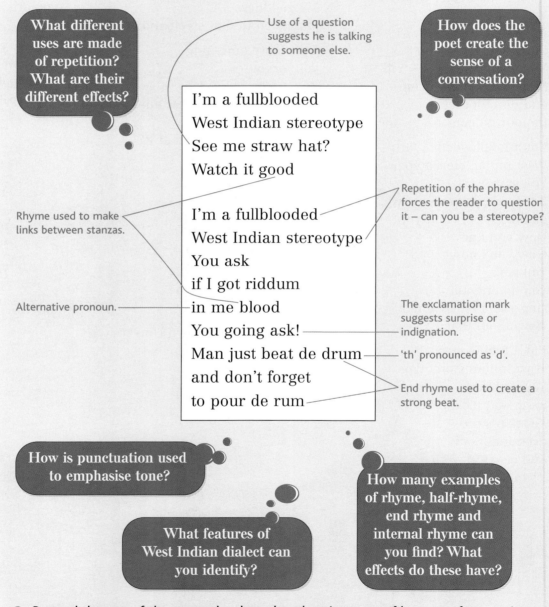

What different uses are made of repetition? What are their different effects?

Use of a question suggests he is talking to someone else.

How does the poet create the sense of a conversation?

I'm a fullblooded
West Indian stereotype
See me straw hat?
Watch it good

I'm a fullblooded
West Indian stereotype
You ask
if I got riddum
in me blood
You going ask!
Man just beat de drum
and don't forget
to pour de rum

Rhyme used to make links between stanzas.

Alternative pronoun.

Repetition of the phrase forces the reader to question it – can you be a stereotype?

The exclamation mark suggests surprise or indignation.

'th' pronounced as 'd'.

End rhyme used to create a strong beat.

How is punctuation used to emphasise tone?

What features of West Indian dialect can you identify?

How many examples of rhyme, half-rhyme, end rhyme and internal rhyme can you find? What effects do these have?

2 Re-read the rest of the poem closely and analyse its range of language features in the same way. Either take notes or highlight and annotate a photocopy of the poem. Use your awareness of the poem's features to help you produce an interesting and lively reading.

Agard starts his poem with the words:

I'm a fullblooded
West Indian stereotype

These are repeated five more times, so clearly he wants the reader to think carefully about them. A 'stereotype' is a standardised image of someone. One of the interesting things about stereotypes is that they don't exist in real life. They are exaggerated images and often not very complimentary. When the speaker of 'Stereotype' claims to be one, he is being ironic and setting a humorous tone for the poem.

Activity 9 ICT

1 Think about how the image of the West Indian stereotype is developed in the course of John Agard's poem. List all the words and phrases that are linked with the West Indian stereotype. If you have a photocopy of the poem, you could highlight these words and phrases or you could draw and annotate the image that is created.

2 How are these stereotypical features made to seem funny? Identify two techniques the poet uses to create humour.

3 Examine the final stanza closely. How has the tone changed here? What point is the speaker making?

4 What does the poet seem to be saying about people's attitudes towards West Indians? Support your ideas with evidence from the text.

5 Why do you think the poet chose to adopt the voice of the stereotype?

Comparing two poems

On first reading, 'A Constable Calls' (see page 35) and 'Stereotype' (see page 39) might appear to be very different. However, on closer reading there are strong similarities between them.

Activity 10 (WS) (ICT)

Make a chart like the one below, then use the work you have done on both poems to complete it. This will help you to identify the main similarities and differences between the poems.

Area for comparison	'A Constable Calls' by Seamus Heaney	'Stereotype' by John Agard
The poet's cultural background		
Subject of poem		
How the subject is linked to the cultural context		
Use of rhyme		
Use of dialect		
How punctuation is used		
How repetition of words and/or sounds is used		
The voice of the poet		

Discovering the character behind the voice

In the three poems you have looked at so far in this unit, the voice of the writer can be clearly heard. That is not always the case, as in the following poem by Robert Browning (1812–1889). Read through the poem carefully before trying to answer the questions at the side.

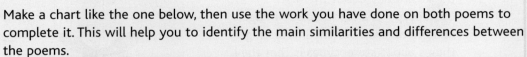

Porphyria's Lover

What scene
is set by the
weather?

The rain set early in tonight,
    The sullen wind was soon awake,
It tore the elm-tops down for spite,
    And did its worst to vex the lake:
5   I listened with heart fit to break.
When glided in Porphyria; straight
    She shut the cold out and the storm,
And kneeled and made the cheerless grate
    Blaze up, and all the cottage warm;
10   Which done, she rose, and from her form
Withdrew the dripping cloak and shawl,
    And laid her soiled gloves by, untied
Her hat and let the damp hair fall,
    And, last, she sat down by my side
15   And called me. When no voice replied,
She put my arm about her waist,
    And made her smooth white shoulder bare,
And all her yellow hair displaced,
    And, stooping, made my cheek lie there,
20   And spread, o'er all, her yellow hair,
Murmuring how she loved me – she
    Too weak, for all her heart's endeavour,
To set its struggling passion free
    From pride, and vainer ties **dissever**,
25   And give herself to me forever.
But passion sometimes would prevail,
    Nor could tonight's gay feast restrain
A sudden thought of one so pale
    For love of her, and all in vain:
30   So, she was come through wind and rain.

What different
things does
Porphyria do
when she
comes in?

What might
her 'vainer
ties' be?

Where has
she been?

Be sure I looked up at her eyes
    Happy and proud; at last I knew
Porphyria worshipped me: surprise
    Made my heart swell, and still it grew
35   While I debated what to do.
That moment she was mine, mine, fair,
    Perfectly pure and good: I found
A thing to do, and all her hair
    In one long yellow string I wound
40   Three times her little throat around,
And strangled her. No pain felt she;
    I am quite sure she felt no pain.
As a shut bud that holds a bee,
    I warily oped her lids: again
45   Laughed the blue eyes without a stain.
And I untightened next the tress
    About her neck; her cheek once more
Blushed bright beneath my burning kiss:
    I propped her head up as before,
50   Only, this time my shoulder bore
Her head, which droops upon it still:
    The smiling rosy little head,
So glad it has its utmost will,
    That all it scorned at once is fled,
55   And I, its love, am gained instead!
Porphyria's love: she guessed not how
    Her darling one wish would be heard.
And thus we sit together now,
    And all night long we have not stirred,
60   And yet God has not said a word!

Robert Browning

What does
he realise?

What does
he do?

How do
they sit?

What does he
think her
'darling one
wish' was?

Why is there
a reference to
God here?

Word bank
dissever – be divided from

'Porphyria's Lover' is a monologue, which means there is one speaker voicing his (or her) thoughts. The speaker is a creation of the poet's imagination. A created character does not have to reflect its creator's own thoughts and feelings.

Activity 11

The poet Robert Browning seems to stand entirely separate from the character he has created in 'Porphyria's Lover' (page 43). But does he have a message for the reader in this poem? In pairs or groups, and using evidence from the poem, talk about whether he is:

◆ warning people to avoid secret love
◆ saying that this kind of love can drive you to desperate acts
◆ suggesting that Porphyria underestimated her lover's feelings, so she deserved to die
◆ hinting that love between different kinds or classes of people is not likely to work
◆ implying that God is tolerant of crimes committed for the sake of love
◆ suggesting that love can never have a happy ending.

Activity 12 ⓦ

Work in pairs. Imagine that after the murder in 'Porphyria's Lover', the speaker is taken to court.

◆ One of you is the prosecution lawyer. You argue that the speaker is wicked and should be severely punished.
◆ The other is the defence lawyer. You argue that the crime was understandable and the punishment should be lenient.

Follow these steps:

Step 1: Make notes for your speech by gathering evidence from the poem about the speaker and build a case either for or against him. It will help you to think about:

◆ where the speaker lives
◆ what you know about Porphyria
◆ which viewpoint the poet would favour
◆ the speaker's actions
◆ the speaker's relationship with Porphyria
◆ the speaker's main characteristics
◆ your own ideas about romantic love
◆ what might be said against the poet's viewpoint.

Your notes should be based on the poem, though you are free to interpret the details in any way you wish.

Step 2: Prepare your speech. As a lawyer you should use standard English to present your case. Your aim is to persuade the jury of your viewpoint about the accused. You will find it useful to include:

◆ pauses
◆ exclamations
◆ rhetorical questions (questions that are asked for effect rather than requiring an answer).

Step 3: Present your case to another pair or a larger group. Ask them to assess your presentation and award you a mark from 1 to 10. They should give reasons for their mark.

You are going to compare two poems, 'Dress Sense' by David Kitchen and 'Dread-lock Style' by Lesley Miranda.

WS 1 Spend 20 minutes reading the poems closely. List points you wish to make and evidence you wish to use. You will be awarded marks for your notes.

Points of comparison	'Dress Sense'	'Dread-lock Style'
The importance of the speaker		
What the poem is about		
How language is used to give the impression of someone talking		
Use of rhyme and/or repetition		
Use of punctuation		
What the poet wants the reader to think		
The effect the poem has on me		
Other points		

15 marks

Dress Sense

You're not going out in that, are you?
I've never seen anything
More ridiculous in my whole life.
You look like you've been dragged
5 Through a hedge backwards
And lost half your dress along the way.

What's wrong with it?
You're asking me what's wrong with that?
Everything: that's what.
10 It's loud, it's common,
It reveals too much of your …
Your … well your 'what you shouldn't be revealing'.

No, I'm not going to explain;
You know very well what I mean, young lady
15 But you choose to ignore
Every single piece of reasonable helpful advice
That you are offered.

It's not just the neckline I'm talking about
– And you can hardly describe it as a neckline,
20 More like a navel-line
If you bother to observe the way that it plunges.
Have you taken a look at the back?
(What little there is of it.)
Have you?

25 Boys are only going to think
One thing
When they see you in that outfit.
Where on earth did you get it?
And don't tell me that my money paid for it
30 Whatever you do.

You found it where?

Well, it probably looked different on her
And, anyway, you shouldn't be going through
Your mother's old clothes.

David Kitchen

Dread-lock Style

Me don't want no hair style
cause me don't want no hair pile
pon me bedroom floor

I say me don't want no hair style
5 cause me don't want no hair pile
pon me bedroom floor

I think I gonna stick to me
dread-lock style
me dread-lock style
10 looking wild wild wild

dem hair gals
putting a dunno what on yuh hair
bunning up yuh scalp
thinking I was born yesterday

15 So I think I gonna stick
to me dread-lock style
me dread-lock style
looking wild wild wild

Lesley Miranda

2 Spend 40 minutes writing your comparison of 'Dress Sense' and 'Dread-lock Style'.
Use the notes you have made to help you to:

◆ point out similarities and differences between the texts

◆ refer to the texts in your answer.

Remember to write in:

◆ standard English   ◆ the present tense.

Below are some useful words and phrases.

◆ In contrast to …   ◆ Whereas …
◆ Similarly …   ◆ In both cases …
◆ They are similar (different) in so far as …   ◆ Both poems …

35 marks
TOTAL 50 marks

Section B ◆ Writing to imagine, explore and entertain
Introduction

In the last two years the focus of your work has been on how to develop narratives and how to use language imaginatively for different effects in a range of poetry. You have experimented with figurative language and with different forms. In the units that follow you will explore a range of forms, including non-fiction. It isn't only in fiction and poetry that language can be shaped imaginatively to entertain readers.

In Unit 5, *Crafting stories*, you will explore some of the ways stories can be shaped and how they can be told from different points of view.

In Unit 6, *Writing to entertain*, you will focus on a range of non-fiction writing, including travel writing and science writing. You will look at how writers exploit language to convey and explore ideas in entertaining ways.

In Unit 7, *Developing ideas in different forms*, you will explore a range of poetic forms. You will think about how things like rhyme and rhythm give shape to ideas.

Unit 8 tests you on the skills you will develop as you work carefully through the three units.

5 Crafting stories

This unit will help you to:
- ◆ explore different kinds of narrative perspective
- ◆ structure stories in different ways
- ◆ develop your range of sentence styles and punctuation.

Perspective

Take a look at the picture below. From your work in art you will know that the trees in the distance are drawn smaller because they look smaller from the place the artist is standing. This is known as 'perspective'. Perspective is about point of view. A narrative perspective is the point of view from which a writer chooses to tell a story.

Most stories are told from one of the following points of view.

1 **First person.** The story is told from the point of view of one of the characters in it. This character is identified as 'I' (first person singular) or 'we' (first person plural). For example:

My footprints track across the faint dew still lying on the grass. My boots crunch heavily on the hard gravel path, and I'm talking to myself as I walk, school bag bumping on my back. But the residents lodged on either side of these avenues won't complain about the noise.

They're dead.

Every one of them.

*from **Whispers in the Graveyard** by Theresa Breslin*

2 **Third Person.** The story is told from the point of view of someone outside of it. Characters are identified as 'she' or 'he' (third person singular) or 'they' (third person plural). For example:

Sky, her little brother Chip, and her parents, had been sleeping in the car for months while they wandered back and forth across the country chasing rumours of work.

They had found some jobs, chopping wood or picking fruit, but nothing which lasted, or which paid enough to feed them all properly, let alone afford somewhere to sleep.

They'd never intended to become **vagrants**.

Word bank
vagrants – people without a home

*from **Throwaways** by Ian Strachan*

3 **Second person.** Writing in the second person, 'you' is used far less often than first and third person. 'You' can be second person singular (one person) or second person plural (more than one person). For example:

You're walking down the street when you get that funny feeling – you know the one – that feeling that you're being watched. Even though you feel a little foolish you have to glance behind you, just to check it out. Usually there's no one there but you still can't shake off the feeling. It nags away at you.

Activity 1 ⓦ

Working with a partner, decide whether the following four extracts are written in the first, second or third person.

1 When I called round at Sally's I showed her the paragraph in the *Westwich Evening News*.

'What do you think of that?' I asked her.

She read it, standing, and with an impatient frown on her pretty face.

'I don't believe it,' she said finally.

*from 'Pawley's Peepholes' by John Wyndham in **The Starlit Corridor***

2 In Stoneygate there was a wilderness. It was an empty space between the houses and the river, where the ancient pit had been. That's where we played Askew's game, the game called Death. We used to gather at the school's gates after the bell had rung. We stood there whispering and giggling. After five minutes, Bobby Carr told us it was time and he led us through the wilderness to Askew's den.

*from **Kit's Wilderness** by David Almond*

3 It was almost December, and Jonas was beginning to be frightened. No. Wrong word, Jonas thought. Frightened meant that deep, sickening feeling of something terrible about to happen. Frightened was the way he had felt a year ago when an unidentified aircraft had overflown the community twice.

*from **The Giver** by Lois Lowry*

4 My father's family name being Pirrip, and my Christian name Philip, my infant tongue could make of both names nothing longer or more explicit than Pip. So, I called myself Pip, and came to be called Pip.

*from **Great Expectations** by Charles Dickens*

Choosing first person

A reader can often relate to an 'I' character. It is like receiving a story first hand. In the following passage the narrator recounts a wartime incident. As you read it, think about what the writer does to convince readers that this is a true eye-witness report.

W
p.200

Surprise encounter

I do not think he had seen us. I think he stood up, perhaps only to ease his aching limbs or rearrange himself in his uncomfortable **slit-trench**. Whatever it was, I think he was more surprised by us than we were by him. And this is
5 what saved us. For luckily he hesitated a moment. Jacob was holding his gun ready to fire, as he had since we set out. But an hour or more of sitting on our garden trolley in the cold and rain had stiffened his already weak body. He did manage to point the gun, but his fingers were so frozen
10 that he fumbled when he tried to fire. As he did so, the German came to his senses and raised his weapon. At that moment Henk let go of the trolley and flung himself at me, pushing me to the ground and falling over me, meaning to protect me. So I did not see what happened next, only
15 heard the shooting of Jacob's gun.

*from **Postcards From No Man's Land** by Aidan Chambers*

Word bank
slit-trench – long narrow dug-out hole

Activity 2

1 In the passage opposite, which phrases used by the narrator show that she is *uncertain* about some of the events?

2 The passage ends: 'I did not see what happened next ...' (lines 14–15). How can the writer let the reader know what happened next if the first person narrator did not see it?

3 The passage gives us an impression of the character of the narrator. What is the attitude of the narrator to an enemy, the German soldier?

Activity 3

Continue the passage opposite by writing a few sentences of your own to let the reader know 'what happened next'. Use the notes below to help you.

◆ The narrator does not see what happened, but you should imagine that Jacob shoots the German soldier.

◆ Your sentences will cover what the narrator finds out when she gets up from the ground.

◆ Look back at your responses to the questions in Activity 2 to help you decide *how* to write the continuation.

◆ Remember, your additions to the story have to be first person, so the narrator can only describe those things she saw or was told.

Writers using a first person narrator

Read the following story called *Momster in the Closet* by Jane Yolen.

Working with a partner, make notes in response to the questions that appear during the story and at the end.

Momster in the Closet

'There's a momster in my closet,' Kenny said. 'I heard him this morning.'

'Grumpf ouff,' Dad said, his mouth full.

'That's nice, dear. Do you want more?' Mom asked.

You see, with Kenny it was something new in that closet every

5 day. At five – 'And a half!' he'd be quick to remind you – he had more imagination than sense. Also, he watched too much TV.

'Come on, squirt,' I said, 'or we'll be late.' I took an extra-long swallow as Kenny shrugged into his backpack. He followed me out of the door.

'Was, too, a momster,' he said.

10 'Monster,' I corrected automatically.

'With long grungy hair. And weird claws. He was nine feet ... no, ten feet tall.'

'Heard all that through the door?' I asked.

That shut him up. Of course, last week it had been a weirdwolf. The time before

it had been a ghould. He didn't know how to pronounce the stuff, but he was convinced
15 they were all there. That must be *some* closet, I thought, and said so out loud.

'Right to Momster Land,' Kenny said.

Kids! I could hardly recall ever being that young. It felt as if I had been a
teenager forever.

---

1 At what stage in the story do you realise this is a first person narrative?

2 What kind of a relationship does the narrator have with Kenny?

3 What impression do you have of the narrator? In particular, is the narrator down to earth
or over-imaginative? Think about the following statements made by the narrator:

◆ *he had more imagination than sense* (lines 5–6)

◆ *he watched too much TV* (line 6)

◆ *I corrected automatically* (line 10).

Now read on.

When we got home, the sun was sitting just below
20 the horizon. Summers are hard around here.
There is just not enough night.

'Come on, squirt,' I said. 'Time for bed.'

'I don't want to go,' Kenny said. 'There's a momster in the closet.'

'You have to. I have to. That's the way of the world,' I said. 'Besides,
25 it's monster. Spelled with an *n* not an *m*.'

'It's got spells, too?' Kenny said. 'Oh, no – it will *really* get me.'

'There's nothing there,' I said, my patience beginning to go. 'Besides, if it threatens
you, just growl back at it and show your teeth like this.' I bared my fangs at him.

Kenny giggled.
30 We went inside. Mom had already settled down, but Dad was still up, sitting in
front of the TV and watching the flag flapping in time to the National Anthem.
It's only a little more exciting than a **test
pattern**. He didn't seem to hear us.

Kenny and I went into the room we
35 shared, and I helped him get undressed.
He still has trouble with the knots in his
shoelaces. I keep asking Mom to find
him a pair of Velcro sneakers.

> **Word bank**
> **test pattern** – still image on a TV screen
> at the end of programme transmission

---

4 What new evidence is there to support the view that the narrator is good-humoured,
kind and considerate?

5 Do you think the narrator is male or female? Why?

Now read to the end of the story.

40 Once we were in our pyjamas and had brushed our teeth, he raced ahead of me
to his bed. He turned for a moment and growled at the closet.

'Fangs for the memory,' I said.

He giggled again, though I don't think he got the joke.

'Last one in is a …' he shouted.

'… rotten …' I prompted.

45 '… corpse!' He made a funny face and lay down. Once his eyes were closed, he
was very still.

I kissed his forehead, moving aside the hair as white-gold as corn silk, and tenderly
closed the lid over him. Then I climbed into my own coffin, pulling it shut before the first
light of day could come streaming through the blinds. Monsters in the closet, indeed! Kenny
50 knew, as I did, that only sunlight or a stake through the heart can really kill a vampire.

I closed my eyes and slept.

Momster in the Closet *by Jane Yolen*

---

6   Now that you have read to the end of the story you will realise that you have been
'tricked' about the narrator. What is the fact about the narrator that isn't fully clear
until the end?

7   Look back to the notes you made for question 3 about what kind of narrator was telling
this story. How does the writer make us think the story is being told by a 'normal'
young person?

Looking at the structure of the story

The plot of *Momster in the Closet* is structured into three main parts:

◆   an opening section, set just before Kenny and the narrator go out
◆   a section where the plot develops, set in the time when they return home before going to bed
◆   a section where the plot is resolved when they are in their pyjamas.

Activity 4

The opening: the writer uses speech to open the story.

1   Look at the three opening lines.
    a   What type of story do they suggest – comic or serious?
    b   The writer could have opened the story with some description of the scene and
        the characters, or with some action. What are the advantages of starting a story
        with a conversation like this?

2   The development: why did the writer choose not to make this more detailed and tell
    us what Kenny and the narrator did while they were out?

3   The resolution: the 'twist' comes at the end of the story in the last four or five sentences.
    But the writer has planted 'clues' as the plot has developed. For example, in the
    development of the story, the words 'There is just not enough night' (line 21) turns out to
    be a hint that the characters move around in the night. What other 'clues' can you find?

Looking at punctuation

The writer of *Momster in the Closet* uses a variety of punctuation to clarify meaning and for effect.

◆ There is a lot of use of speech in the story.
◆ There are some exclamation marks (!), which are used to emphasise something.
◆ There is some use of ellipsis (...).
◆ There are some dashes, which can be used like 'strong' commas.

Activity 5 (WS) (ICT)

1 Copy the sentence below, then write brief notes in each space to explain the purpose of the punctuation marks.

The mark indicates the start of what is spoken.

"Come on, squirt," I said, "or we'll be late." (line 7)

2 How does the use of the exclamation mark after 'Kids!' (line 17) affect how you say the word and what the character means when she uses the word?

3 Look at the following use of ellipsis by the writer and write down an explanation of why it has been used. Kenny, getting a little carried away, says:

'He was nine feet ... no, ten feet tall.' (line 11)

4 Look at the following two examples of the use of dashes. Then write a brief explanation of why the writer has used them.

At five – 'And a half!' he'd be quick to remind you – he had more imagination than sense. (lines 5–6)

'Oh, no – it will really get me.' (line 26)

Tricking the reader

Sometimes, stories 'trick' the reader into thinking something about the narrator. For example, the narrator could turn out to be:

◆ an animal ◆ a different age or gender from what the reader thought ◆ a ghost.

Activity 6

Write your own short story in which you trick the reader. You should:

◆ use a first person narrator
◆ include some speech in your story
◆ use a range of punctuation
◆ think carefully about the stages of your story: opening, development and resolution.

Step 1: Think what your trick will be. You can choose one from the list given above, or you can use one of your own.

Step 2: Think about how to 'convince' your reader of what your narrator is like.

The narrator in the *Momster in the Closet* was made convincingly 'normal':

◆ She was an 'ordinary' teenager using teen slang and expressions (*'Come on, squirt,' I said* – line 7).
◆ She had a sense of humour (*'Fangs for the memory,' I said* – line 41).
◆ She was surrounded by 'ordinary' things (dad, mum, TV, sneakers – lines 2, 3, 6, 38).
◆ She had a caring nature (*I kissed his forehead, moving aside the hair as white-gold as corn silk, and tenderly* … – line 47), which is not what we expect from a vampire.

Step 3: Build in clues for the reader. For example, if you were writing a story in which the narrator turned out to be a cat you might write something like this:

> 'There, I think you'll like that.'
> She smiled as she left me to it. I've got her well-trained. She knows what I like. All right, it's usually out of a tin but I'm not complaining. If you're out all night like I am you want a good meal in the morning.

The mention of tins and being out all night are clues that the narrator is a cat.

Step 4: Write a first draft. Regularly re-read it and make amendments. Show your draft to a partner and ask him or her to respond to the following questions.

◆ Does the opening make you want to read on?
◆ Can you see the 'clues' planted in the story before the surprise ending?
◆ Is there a range of effective punctuation? Consider the use of exclamation marks, dashes and ellipsis as well as commas, full stops and speech marks.

Step 5: Consider what your partner says and write your final draft.

Multiple narration

Some stories may be told by more than one narrator. This can bring variety to writing because different narrators have different 'voices'. They also have a different perspective on events.

Having more than one narrator can allow a writer to structure a story in an interesting way. In Robert Swindells's novel *Stone Cold* there are two narrators – one of them is a seventeen-year-old boy who becomes homeless. Read this part of his story. As you read, think about what kind of a character the narrator is.

Stone Cold

p.201

I wasn't out every night, back then. That was the one good thing about it. Once or twice a week I'd show up at my sister's for a bath, a meal and a decent night's sleep. Trouble was, I was getting scruffier and scruffier, which happens if you sleep in your clothes, and Chris, Carole's feller, got resentful of my visits. He didn't actually say
5   anything to me, but I could see it in his eyes and hear it in his tone of voice, and I knew Carole must be catching hell from him every time I'd been there. So, what with one thing and another, I decided it was time to move on.

Sounds good, right? Time to move on. Reminds you of all those old
songs about the restless character who hates to stay too long in one
10 place. He meets a girl who falls in love with him, but after a while he
hears the old highway calling and so he slings his bed-roll over his
shoulder and moves on, leaving the girl to grieve. Dead romantic, eh?

Forget it. Sad, is what it is. Sad and scary. You're leaving a place
you know and heading into the unknown with nothing to protect
15 you. No money. No prospect of work. No address where folks will
make you welcome. You're going to find yourself living among hard,
violent people, some of whom are **deranged**. You're going to be at
risk every minute, day and night. Especially night. There are guys
so desperate or so crazy, they'll knife you or batter your head in
20 for your sleeping-bag and the **coppers** you've got in your pocket.
There are some who'll try to get in your sleeping-bag with you,
because you're a nice-looking lad with soft skin and no stubble.
And there's nowhere you can run to, because
nobody cares. Nobody gives a damn. You're
25 just another **dosser**, and one dosser
more or less makes no difference.

*from **Stone Cold** by Robert Swindells*

Word bank

deranged – mentally unstable
coppers – small change
dosser – vagrant or tramp

Activity 7 WS

1 Copy the chart below. Then use it to make notes about the language the writer gets
the narrator, Link, to use.

	Link	Examples
Vocabulary (the kinds of words he uses)	◆ Uses straightforward words with some slang ◆ Is down to earth	For example, 'feller'
Expression (the way he puts words together)	◆ Uses some very short sentences ◆ Tries to put the reader into his shoes	

2 Using the notes you have made, write a few sentences about what kind of narrator
Link seems to be. Begin with:

From what the narrator tells us and from the way he expresses himself, I imagine the
narrator to …

The other narrator in *Stone Cold* is very different. His name is Shelter. He dislikes homeless people and kills them.

It's like parachuting. Get the first jump over and it becomes routine, but you mustn't get complacent. Check your equipment every time. Run through procedures. Know what's what. Don't fall into any traps.

There's a trap serial killers fall into, namely, the trap of pattern. There's something the
5 same about each of their killings, and this tells the law that it's the same person doing them. It also helps the police by saying something about the killer. For example, if all his victims are Mexican they know they're probably looking for a bloke who hates Mexicans. If all the bodies are found in underground stations, they're after someone who hangs around underground stations. It's a trap, see? A trap of the killer's own making, because
10 it narrows the field.

I've got to be particularly careful about this. I can't help making a pattern, because all of my clients are dossers. Bound to be. Of course, they're not going to find bodies, in underground stations or anywhere else. I'm not that daft. But there is this unavoidable pattern, so what I have to do is create as much variety as possible without straying
15 beyond the borders of my appointed task.

*from **Stone Cold** by Robert Swindells*

Activity 8

1 Copy out a chart like the one you made for Link (see page 57). Then make notes about the language the writer gets Shelter to use.

2 How are Shelter's attitudes towards 'dossers' different from Link's?

3 It turns out that Shelter has a military background. What *vocabulary* does he use that suggests this background?

4 Shelter refers to his victims as 'clients' (line 12). Why has the writer decided to get him to use this word?

5 Are there any other ways in which you can tell this passage is by a different narrator?

Activity 9 (WS) (ICT)

Write your own story using two narrators, using the steps below to guide you. Your story will be entitled 'The Argument'. In your story you should:

◆ create two different first person narrators using the skills you have developed in this unit

◆ tell 'the argument' from two different points of view.

Step 1: Decide on the plot. Think about your own experience. Brainstorm a list of the kinds of things that lead you into arguments or that you see leading other people to argue. What leads to arguments between friends? Family? Strangers?

When you have a short list, review it and, with the help of a partner, decide which idea could be explored further in your story. Avoid anything that is very complicated.

Using a chart like the one below, write down the details of the argument you choose to develop.

The argument is between ...
A fifteen-year-old girl and her mother. The girl was meant to be home from a Saturday night party at 11 pm. When she didn't arrive by 11.30 pm, her mum went to the party to get her. The girl was embarrassed.

One side of the argument is ...	The other side is ...
The girl was enjoying herself and just lost track of the time. She felt she'd been treated like a little kid by her mother.	The mum was very worried and thought her daughter had been selfish.

Step 2: Choose your narrators. Look back at how the writers in *Momster in the Closet* and *Stone Cold* 'created' ways for their narrators to express themselves. Then think about how your two narrative 'voices' can be made different. For example, in a story about an argument in a shop, one narrator could be well educated and the other not very literate.

Draw a chart like the one below. Then use it to help you create two different voices.

	Well 'educated'	Not very literate
Vocabulary	◆ Some polysyllabic words ◆ Some use of technical jargon ◆ Few ellipses – keeps sentences whole	◆ Mostly monosyllabic words ◆ Slang ◆ Lots of shortened words
Expression	◆ Uses complex sentences with frequent use of commas and semicolons	◆ Simple short sentences with limited range of punctuation

Step 3: Break down the plot.

◆ The argument will already have taken place, so it will be written in the past tense.

◆ Your two narrators will give their versions of what happened – what led up to the argument and how they both feel about it.

◆ There will only be two sections. You need to decide which narrator begins, and who has the last word.

In the story about the teenager late home from the party, you might decide to sympathise with the girl and make her mum seem over-protective. If so, you could begin with the girl's version of events, which show there was nothing for her mother to worry about. This could be followed with the mother's version, so that readers then understand her over-reaction.

a **The opening.** Once you have decided which narrator to begin with, you need to make the opening interesting for a reader. For example, you might open your story with speech, like the writer of *Momster in the Closet*. In the story about the teenager late home from the party, this might read something like:

> *'Mum … What? What are you doing here?' I couldn't believe it. How could she do this to me? When she told me to get in the car I just flipped. I'd been having a really good time …*

b **The development.** When you change to the second narrator, you need to think carefully about what to include. Readers have already been told the story by the first narrator, so you should avoid repeating things such as the same piece of dialogue.

c **The resolution.** The resolution of your story should be satisfying for your readers, leaving them with something to think about. For example, in the party story the girl's account could end with 'I hate her!' and the mother's version could end with 'She's my daughter: I love her.' These would give readers something to think about.

Step 4: Write out a first draft of your complete story. Then show it to your partner. Ask if s/he can see what you have done to make the 'voices' different. Have you varied:

◆ the vocabulary

◆ the expression

◆ the content?

Step 5: Write a final draft. Consider what your partner has said and make any changes to your story. Then ask your partner to read your finished draft, looking in particular at how well you have created two distinct 'voices'.

6 Writing to entertain

This unit will help you to:

- ◆ write a range of non-fiction
- ◆ explore how non-fiction texts can convey information in an entertaining way
- ◆ consider the structure of paragraphs
- ◆ use language in imaginative ways.

Journalism

Newspapers contain many different kinds of writing about a variety of topics. Because it is essential for newspapers to make money by attracting readers it is important that they convey various kinds of information in ways that entertain different kinds of readers.

The following piece of writing is from the travel supplement of a Sunday newspaper. It is part of a feature on different phrase books, and eventually offers advice on the merits and faults of a range of phrase books. As you read it, keep a note of what the writer's ideas about phrase books are.

Lost for words

Are phrase books a waste of time? Joanne O'Connor puts five of the best to the test while on holiday in Portugal.

'Pod rerkoomayndarmer algoonsh pratoosh rerzhyoonighsh?'
I ask hopefully. The waiter smiles with the air of one who has suffered much and turns on his heel. Moments later, he returns with a menu in English. 'The speciality is grilled sardines,' he
5 says. I hide my Portuguese phrase book under the table. 'OK, I'll have that.' And then, inexplicably, I order a glass of white wine in Spanish, but with a French accent. That'll show him.

He returns with a huge **carafe** of wine. My dilemma: whether to explain shamefacedly that I only wanted a glass, which he
10 would have understood if I hadn't tried to show off by speaking Spanish, or pretend I meant to order it and drink the whole carafe. I decide the latter is easier.

Having just spent a weekend in Lisbon putting a handful of Portuguese phrase books through their paces, I can confirm that,
15 where foreign languages are concerned, a little bit of knowledge is a dangerous thing. Apart from anything else, there is something fundamentally naff about using a phrase book. Like guide books, cameras and sunburn, they confer on the user an instant badge of shame: 'Look at me everyone, I'm a tourist.' Surely it's better to be
20 lost and misunderstood than causing patisserie queue rage as you insist on looking up the word for custard tart.

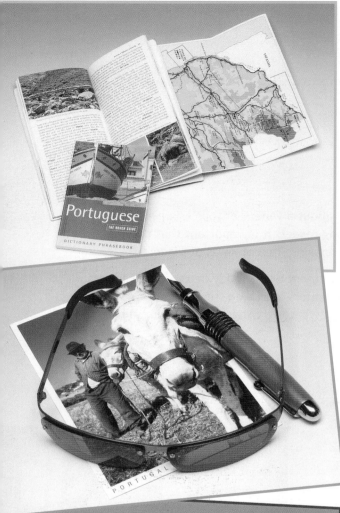

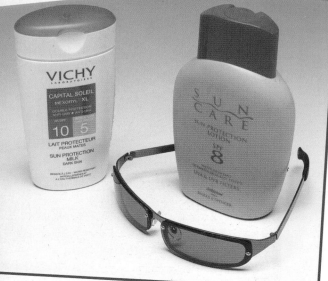

You can try to get around this by secretly swotting up on a few key phrases and keeping the book out of sight, but even this can backfire horribly. Before
25 joining the ticket queue in the metro, I rehearsed: 'A return ticket to Oriente, please', only to be told in Portuguese that this particular metro line was still under construction (though obviously I didn't understand this was what he was saying at the time).
30 By the time you have looked this one up in your phrase book, a) you will have been lynched by an angry mob, b) the man behind the counter will have pulled down the blind and gone home, or c) if you are really lucky the line will have been completed. The
35 moral of this story: speak perfect Portuguese to people and they will answer you in perfect Portuguese, which is not much good if you can't speak the language.

Still, you can't help but be touched by the optimism of the publishers who hopefully throw in chapters
40 headed 'Making friends' and 'Socialising'. Who are they trying to kid? If you have to look up the words for 'I'd really like to see you again' then it's unlikely your **sparkling repartee** will have won you a second date. But if you do get lucky, **Lonely Planet** boldly
45 goes where no phrase book has gone before, with a section on the language of love from 'Oh baby, don't stop' (which seems to rely on the dubious premise that you have your phrase book to hand at all times) to 'Why don't we live together?'
50 I suppose we should be grateful that most phrase books have finally acknowledged that our holidays don't revolve entirely around the bus station or the grocer. But the content of some of the books tends to be a bit hit and miss.

*from the 'Escape' section of the **Observer**, 12 August 2001*

Word bank

carafe – a jug
sparkling repartee – witty remarks
Lonely Planet – the name of a series of phrase/travel books

Looking at techniques

The writer uses a number of techniques to make her writing entertaining.

Engaging the reader

The opening of the passage on page 61 (lines 1–2)
shows how non-fiction and fiction share
characteristics – for example, a 'hook' to
get their readers interested straightaway.

Activity 1 ICT

Working with a partner, discuss the following questions and note down your ideas.

1 Why do you think the writer of the article began it with words that aren't English?
   How does it help to hook readers and get them to read on?

2 The opening two paragraphs of this article are written in the present tense even
   though they are things that happened in the past. Why do you think the writer
   chose to write them like this?

3 The opening three paragraphs are written in the first person, telling the story of
   what happened in Lisbon. This changes, largely, to the second person – 'you' – in
   the following paragraphs. What are the reasons for this?

Making it interesting and easy to follow

Structure is another technique used to make this writing entertaining. The article consists of a
headline, a sub-headline and seven paragraphs of writing.

Activity 2

Work on the following with a partner. Make notes of your responses as you work.

1 Look at the headline, sub-headline and first two paragraphs of the article. Which one
   tells you clearly what the *purpose* of the piece of writing is?

2 Paragraphs are used in a piece of writing to separate ideas. The first two paragraphs
   on page 61 tell a little story, in two stages. What is the main idea and purpose of
   each of the next four paragraphs? Sum up each paragraph in a few words.

3 The writer keeps the writing flowing through paragraphs by using key words and phrases
   in the opening sentences that link to the previous paragraph. For example, in 'You can
   try to get around this by …' (line 22), the phrase 'get around this' clearly links back to
   what 'this' is. Look at the opening sentences of other paragraphs in the article. Then note
   down the key words and phrases that link the sentence to the previous paragraph.

Connecting sentences within paragraphs

In addition to structuring paragraphs the writer has carefully structured and connected the sentences within paragraphs.

The sentence opening	Connections
Having just spent a weekend in Lisbon ... (line 13)	The opening sets the time and place and states a point of view
Apart from anything else ... (line 16)	This gives a supporting piece of evidence ...
Like ... they ... (lines 17 and 18)	which is further developed by an example
Surely ... (line 19)	A conclusive final illustration

You can use these kinds of sentence connections in your own writing.

Activity 3

1 Look at the paragraph below, and concentrate on the opening words of each sentence.

> Having just been to the school canteen, I would like to say that the food isn't wonderful. Apart from anything else, it is not very healthy. Like fast food outlets, much of what is on offer contains a lot of fat. Surely mum's wholemeal sandwiches are a better bet.

2 Now use the same four sentence starters to write your own paragraph about a subject of your own choice.

Including complex sentences to connect ideas

Look again at the second paragraph of the article that begins on page 61. The author uses interesting sentence structures to connect ideas. A long sentence is followed by a much shorter sentence.

Colon: a punctuation mark used to indicate an extended explanation or that an example is to follow.

Second part of the sentence construction, which joins the two alternatives 'whether ... or'.

> My dilemma: whether to explain shamefacedly that I only wanted a glass, which he would have understood if I hadn't tried to show off by speaking Spanish, or pretend I meant to order it and drink the whole carafe. I decide the latter is easier.

First part of the sentence construction 'whether ... or'.

Relative clause that drops more information into the sentence, surrounded by commas.

Passage written in present tense to add to humour and make it snappier.

Activity 4

You can use a complex sentence structure in your own writing by identifying the skeleton of the sentence. Copy the structure on page 64 to build up two sentences with your own ideas for content. It could be any dilemma or problem.

My problem: whether …

Bringing humour to writing

The writer of the article that begins on page 61 uses humour to mock herself and the idea of using phrase books. She does this through:

◆ choice of vocabulary ◆ sarcasm ◆ exaggeration.

Choice of vocabulary

Sometimes the humorous mocking tone can be seen in the choice of words. For example, 'patisserie queue rage' (line 20) is humorous because it reminds you of 'road rage', a well-known phenomenon. The idea that there could be raging, bad-tempered incidents in a cake shop is absurd.

Sarcasm

The writer mocks herself in the opening two paragraphs: she tells a story that makes her seem slightly ridiculous. For example, 'Moments later, he returns with a menu in English' (lines 3–4) shows that her attempt at Portuguese has only shown her up as being English.

Exaggeration

The writer uses this technique in the form of a list in the article.

Activity 5 🖳

1 In what way are the following choices of vocabulary intended to be humorous?
   a 'your sparkling repartee' (line 43).
   b 'Pod rerkoomayndarmer algoonsh pratoosh rerzhyoonighsh?' I ask hopefully (lines 1–2).

2 Read the penultimate paragraph (lines 38–49). What is the writer being sarcastic about and mocking in this paragraph? Choose and explain two phrases from this paragraph that reveal her mocking tone.

3 What does the writer exaggerate in the paragraph beginning 'By the time ...' (line 30)? Why does she do it?

Activity 6

Using the steps below as a guide, write a passage of three or four paragraphs in which you mock something.

◆ Begin with a little story intended to 'hook' your reader.
◆ Express opinions about your subject matter.
◆ Use complex sentences to link ideas.
◆ Use clear, helpful paragraphing to show the different stages of your thinking.
◆ Use words and expressions designed to be humorous.
◆ Use a mocking tone with sarcasm and exaggeration.

Step 1: Choose a subject that you have some knowledge of. For example, you could mock school uniform or public transport.

If you were to choose public transport as your theme:

◆ your 'hook' might be about getting caught in the rain in town
◆ your opinion might be that it is very poor
◆ your complex sentence might look something like this:

My dilemma: whether to suffer the discomfort of a vandalised seat on the bus, which might leave chewing gum stuck to my trousers and pen on my jacket, or walk the long distance to the precinct and risk being caught in a torrential downpour. I decide the former won't result in three weeks off work with hypothermia.

Step 2: Choose what to mock. For example, if you choose to mock school uniform there might be two aspects of it that you mock:

◆ the idea that it makes everyone look the same – something that just isn't true
◆ the idea that making people dress the same somehow leads to a better school.

Step 3: Write your 'hook'. Decide on a little story you could use to hook your reader.

Step 4: Complete a first draft of your story. When you have written your 'hook', write two or three more paragraphs in draft form in which you mock two or three different aspects of your subject.

Step 5: When you have written a first draft ask a partner to help you evaluate it to see if it meets the following criteria.

◆ Do the sentences in each paragraph 'connect' with each other?
◆ Do the paragraphs 'flow' into each other? Are there words in the opening sentence of the paragraph that link back to the previous one?
◆ Have you used a complex sentence as shown in Step 1 and practised in Activity 4?
◆ Are there examples of vocabulary and expression used for humorous effect?
◆ Is there any use of sarcasm?

Step 6: Revise your piece of writing in the light of what you and your partner discuss. Write a final draft.

Developing a comic approach

The writer of the article 'Lost for words' (pages 61–62) was focusing on phrase books and whether they are useful. As you read the following extract from Bill Bryson's *Neither Here Nor There*, decide what you think this writer's purpose is. He describes an experience in Rome.

Devastating parking

I love the way the Italians park. You turn any street corner in Rome and it looks as if you've just missed a parking competition for blind people. Cars are pointed in every direction, half on the pavements and half off, facing in, facing sideways, blocking garages and side streets and phone boxes, fitted into spaces so tight that the only
5 possible way out would be through the sun roof. Romans park their cars the way I would park if I had just spilled a beaker of **hydrochloric acid** on my lap.

I was strolling along the **Via Sistina** one morning when a **Fiat Croma** shot past and screeched to a smoky halt a hundred feet up the road. Without pause the driver lurched into reverse and came barrelling backwards down the street in the direction
10 of a parking space that was precisely the length of his Fiat, less two and a half feet. Without slowing even fractionally, he veered the car into the space and crashed resoundingly into a parked **Renault**.

Nothing happened for a minute. There was just the hiss of escaping steam. Then the driver leaped from his car, gazed in profound disbelief at the devastation before
15 him – crumpled metal, splintered tail lights, the exhaust pipe of his own car limply grazing the pavement – and regarded it with as much mystification as if it had dropped on him from the sky. Then he did what I suppose almost any Italian would do. He kicked the Renault in the side as hard as he could, denting the door, punishing its absent owner for having the **gall** to park it there, then leaped back in his Fiat and
20 drove off as madly as he had arrived, and peace returned once again to the Via Sistina, apart from the occasional clank of a piece of metal dropping off the stricken Renault. No one but me batted an eye.

*from **Neither Here Nor There**
by Bill Bryson*

> ### Word bank
> **hydrochloric acid** – a very strong acid
> **Via Sistina** – the Sistina road
> **Fiat Croma** – a type of car
> **Renault** – a type of car
> **gall** – cheek

In many ways there is nothing funny about the event described on the previous page. It is the writer's approach to it that is humorous.

The incident itself is quite simple. The writer sees someone trying to reverse his car into a space that is too small, collide with the car behind, get out and kick the damaged car, then drive off. The writer:

◆ sees humour in this and writes with a comic perspective
◆ uses language in particular ways for comic effects.

Activity 7 ⬥ICT⬥

1 Discuss the following with a partner and make notes of your responses.
   a What does the writer see as amusing about the way Italians park?
   b What does he think is funny about the incident with the Fiat Croma?

2 The writer likes to describe things in comic ways by using figurative language. He develops entertaining comparisons. Look at each example below and, working with your partner, write different comparisons that would also be comic. In each case you need to change the underlined section.

> a ... it looks as if _you've just missed a parking competition for blind people_ (lines 1–2).
> b Romans park their cars the way _I would park if I had just spilled a beaker of hydrochloric acid on my lap_ (lines 5–6).
> c ... regarded it with as much mystification as if _it had dropped on him from the sky_ (lines 16–17).

3 The comic drama of the second paragraph on page 67 is created through clever use of language. With your partner:
   a list the verbs used by the writer to create a comic picture of how fast and recklessly the Italian drives the Fiat Croma
   b imagine you observed an accident that was caused by a car travelling very slowly rather than fast.
   Write only three or four sentences, but use a number of carefully chosen verbs to emphasise the slowness of the vehicle. You could begin:

> 'I was jogging down ...

How travel writers use language

Writing does not have to be funny to be entertaining. Travel writers find words to make places and people interesting. Read the description opposite of part of an African journey by Christina Dodwell. As you read it think about the kinds of language the writer uses to let the reader share the experience of an exotic place.

p.200

Exotic dawn

As the sun rose we floated off downriver. Dawn in an **iridescent** world, hushed as the inner wall of a shell. Mist floating suspended in a never-ending sky, vulnerable as all beautiful things. The water was like glass; purple flowering hyacinth cast reflections as true as life; we drifted silently; it was not for us to
5 disturb the tranquillity. The wide flat river went snaking through dense tangled mighty forest; trees tall and majestic, roped together with knotted vines, strung with white flowering creeper; branches hung shaggy with green trailing lichen, and enshrouded in cobweb; straight trees with pale luminous pinky-yellow bark, short squat trees with leaves like fans, or feathers; trees with leaves the size
10 of umbrellas; gnarled old and crooked trees; immense trees 100 feet tall with roots like the fins of rocket ships; impenetrable dark undergrowth; monkeys fighting and thunder rumbling; parrots and hornbills flying overhead; hot and sultry sun; the smell of sweating earth in the forest, and the perfume of flowers hanging heavily in the air.

*Christina Dodwell, from **The Virago Book of Women Travellers***

Word bank
iridescent – shining

Activity 8

1 In this passage, the author has written one very long sentence beginning, 'The wide flat river' (line 5).

   a Which punctuation mark does the author use to separate the different parts of that sentence?

   b Why do you think the author chose to write it that way instead of breaking it up into several shorter sentences?

2 The author uses a mixture of adjectives and similes to describe the trees. Sometimes the description involves the simple use of adjectives, such as in 'gnarled old and crooked trees' (line 10). However, there is also a pattern using the preposition 'with'. One example of this is 'straight trees with pale luminous pinky-yellow bark' (line 8). What other examples of this pattern can you find?

3 Finally, like Bill Bryson (see page 67), the author uses figurative language to bring the description to life.

   One example is 'The water was like glass' (line 3). This is an interesting image for a number of reasons. The author seems to suggest it's like a mirror, so that you get perfect reflections in it. That makes it sound crystal clear and beautiful. But it might also make you think of how fragile glass is. The author uses the word 'vulnerable' just before (line 3). It's as though this is a paradise that could easily be shattered. Choose three of the author's images and write about their effectiveness.

Activity 9

Think about the travel writing you have studied on pages 67 and 69, and the skills of the two writers. Then write a short descriptive passage of a place you know well. Use two or three paragraphs to bring the place to life for a reader. Use the following steps to help you.

Step 1: Choose a place. Where would you like to set your piece of writing?

◆ Is it your home town?

◆ Or is it a place you have visited?

Step 2: Choose a style of writing. Will you write a word picture like Christina Dodwell? Or will you base your piece of writing on an event, like Bill Bryson?

Step 3: Make a plan. Think about how you will break your piece into paragraphs. For example, Bill Bryson begins by expressing an opinion. Then he tells a story to explain that opinion. The story is broken down into its separate parts.

Step 4: Write a first draft. Use some of the techniques you have worked on in previous activities, such as:

◆ connecting paragraphs

◆ using figurative language

◆ using complex sentences to connect ideas.

Step 5: Revise your first draft. Sometimes it is difficult to make yourself change a first draft. To help you focus, rewrite your second paragraph. Keep the same idea but change some of your words.

◆ Open it with a sentence that links it to the previous paragraph, but make it a different sentence from your original.

◆ Find other ways of expressing your ideas in following sentences.

◆ Compare the results with your original.

Here is an example of an original piece of writing followed by an alternative version.

> **Original version:** The ring road is a nightmare. It is an ugly sprawl of dull concrete. It circles the city centre and makes it difficult for anyone to enter and find the place they are looking for. Drivers often get lost and find themselves endlessly going round in circles.
>
> **Alternative version:** The ring road is a nightmare. Like some hideous concrete snake it wraps itself round the city centre. Entering the city centre becomes a dangerous challenge. Some fail the challenge and find themselves driving, endlessly, around in circles.

Step 6: Compare your two paragraphs. With the help of a partner, decide which one is most effective. Look at the rest of your draft in a similar way.

Step 7: Once you are happy with your revisions, write a final draft of your piece.

Science writing

You might expect writing about the subject of science and the environment to be largely factual and 'dry'. But science writers can use language in the same imaginative ways as travel writers to convey their ideas in entertaining ways. The extract below is from the opening of a book published in 1964. The book had a great influence on the second part of the twentieth century. As you read it think about what other kinds of writing it reminds you of.

Silent Spring

There was once a town in the heart of America where all life seemed to live in harmony with its surroundings. The town lay in the midst of a checkerboard of prosperous farms, with fields of grain and hillsides of orchards where, in spring, white clouds of bloom drifted above the green fields. In autumn, oak and maple and
5 birch set up a blaze of colour that flamed and flickered across a backdrop of pines. Then foxes barked in the hills and deer silently crossed the fields, half hidden in the mists of the autumn mornings.

Along the roads, laurel, viburnum and alder, great ferns and wildflowers delighted the traveller's eye through much of the year. Even in winter the roadsides were places
10 of beauty, where countless birds came to feed on the berries and on the seed heads of the dried weeds rising above the snow. The countryside was, in fact, famous for the abundance and variety of its bird life, and when the flood of **migrants** was pouring through in spring and autumn people travelled from great distances to observe them. Others came to fish the streams, which flowed clear and cold out of the hills and
15 contained shady pools where trout lay. So it had been from the days many years ago when the first settlers raised their houses, sank their wells, and built their barns.

Then a strange blight crept over the area and everything began to change. Some evil spell had settled on the community: mysterious **maladies** swept the flocks of chickens; the cattle and sheep sickened and died. Everywhere was a shadow of death.
20 The farmers spoke of much illness among their families. In the town the doctors had become more and more puzzled by new kinds of sickness appearing among their patients. There had been several sudden and unexplained deaths, not only among adults but even among children, who would be stricken suddenly while at play and die within a few hours. …

25 The roadsides, once so attractive, were now lined with browned and withered vegetation as though swept by fire. These, too, were silent, deserted by all living things. Even the streams were now lifeless. Anglers no longer visited them, for all the fish had died.

In the gutters under the eaves and between the shingles of the roofs, a white **granular** powder still showed a few patches; some weeks before it had
30 fallen like snow upon the roofs and the lawns, the fields and streams.

No **witchcraft**, no enemy action had silenced the rebirth of new life in this stricken world. The people had done it themselves.

*from **Silent Spring** by Rachel Carson*

Word bank
migrants – travelling birds
maladies – illnesses
granular – grainy
witchcraft – black magic

Activity 10 ⓦⓢ

1 'Silent Spring' is from a chapter called 'A fable for tomorrow'. The writer uses language in particular ways to suggest that this is a fable, fairy tale or myth. She begins, for example, 'There was once a town' (line 1), which is like 'Once upon a time …'. What other words and phrases can you find that show the writer is writing in the style of a fable or myth? List them, using your own experience of fairy tales to help you.

2 In the first two paragraphs of the passage, the writer is describing a beautiful picture. 'There was once' suggests a beautiful world that existed in the past. The writer chooses words carefully to create the right kind of atmosphere, as the example below shows.

> 'In autumn, oak and maple and birch set up a blaze of colour that flamed and flickered across a backdrop of pines' (lines 4–5).

   ◆ She names many natural things (four kinds of tree in the same sentence).
   ◆ She uses 'blaze of colour', which is a vivid metaphor suggesting the beautiful reds and oranges of autumn.
   ◆ She uses the alliteration 'flamed and flickered' to draw attention to the metaphor of fire. It also makes the picture dynamic as though it is moving.
   ◆ She uses 'backdrop of pines', which sounds like a stage setting making the scene dramatic.

   Choose another sentence from the first two paragraphs that is particularly effective. Explain its effectiveness in a similar way to the model above.

3 The final paragraph contains only two sentences. The first sentence builds the suspense, leaving you wondering who or what could have done this terrible thing? It is a statement that has a question behind it.

   The final sentence is a killer blow. A surprise. Why, from what has gone before, is the answer to the 'mystery' so surprising?

4 The writer isn't really writing a fable. She is attacking the use of pesticides. Why do you think she decided to use the style of a fable or fairy tale? Put the following possible reasons in order with the most reasonable at the top.

   ◆ It's just 'different' and makes it interesting.
   ◆ It's because she's not telling the truth.
   ◆ It helps her to show how amazing the effect of insecticides has been – like a dark force from the world of fables.
   ◆ Stories 'hook' readers and we all know fairy tales about powerful forces, so we can relate to them.

The writer of 'Silent Spring' which begins on page 71 is attacking the widespread use of pesticides. She suggests there was once a lovely world that has been spoiled. She uses language in very particular ways to create a very descriptive fairy-tale style because in fairy tales you find there is often an 'evil' force that threatens something lovely – think of *Snow White* and *Little Red Riding Hood*.

The writer uses the following conventions of a fable or fairy tale.

◆ Stock phrases like 'There was once' (line 1) and 'evil spell' (line 18).

◆ Very descriptive language to emphasise beauty and goodness on one side, and ugliness and evil on the other.

◆ It is written in the past tense.

Activity 11

1 Use similar methods to write two brief paragraphs of your own. Think of a place that could change from loveliness to ugliness. For example:

◆ a green field site that becomes a housing development

◆ a house before and after a party.

2 In the first paragraph create a 'perfect', fabulous world that has been spoiled by one of the circumstances above. Begin with 'Once upon a time ...' or 'There was once ...'.

3 In the second paragraph, write a description of the 'spoiled' feature. What you write should sound like a fable or fairy tale.

This unit will help you to:
◆ write in different forms of poetry
◆ explore how form shapes meaning.

Writing poetry: being aware of different forms

Whenever you have an idea you wish to explore in writing, you are faced with a great range of choices. How will you express your idea? You could jot something in a diary, write a letter, type an e-mail, or write a poem or story. Ideas may be developed in a variety of ways.

Texts come in all shapes and sizes – some of them very short! In his selection of poems *Short and Sweet*, Simon Armitage includes the following, which is the shortest poem.

On Going to Meet a Zen Master in the Kyushu Mountains and Not Finding Him

For A.G.

Don Paterson

The poem consists of only the title. Zen is a form of Buddhism and the Kyushu Mountains are in Japan, where Zen Buddhism is especially important. There is a kind of absurd joke in the poem – about someone searching for the meaning of life and simply not finding it.

Can you think of other ideas for titles of poems in which the absence of any other lines might make a point? Here is an example.

MEMORIES OF LAST NIGHT'S REVISION: A POEM

This is intended as a joke, but it may be possible to make a serious point about an issue – for example:

THE WHALE'S FUTURE: A POEM

Activity 1

Write three poems that consist of only a title. Write a mixture of the funny and the serious.

Keeping it short

It's often more effective to write very concisely as the poem below shows.

Poem Against Capital Punishment

I live in the capital
and it's punishment

Roger McGough

The poem is based on looking at a fairly common phrase in a new way. Interesting results can be achieved by trying something as simple and short as that.

Activity 2 (WS) (ICT)

1 Write three brief poems based on a new look at some of the following phrases.

- ◆ Channel-hopping
- ◆ ring road
- ◆ computer mouse
- ◆ fast food
- ◆ express checkout
- ◆ body clock
- ◆ hi-fi
- ◆ crime figures

You need to let your mind think over the possibilities. Here is an example based on 'Hi-Fi'.

> HI-FI
> Hi!
> Have you seen Fee?
> Or Fo?
> Or, whatsisname, um?

2 Share your results with a partner. What does your partner think works well in your poem. Could anything be improved?

Adding shape through rhyme

In poetry, ideas can be shaped in a variety of ways. An idea can be given more impact through the use of rhyme. Short poems can be made effective with the use of strong rhythm and rhyme to give shape and add punch to the words. Below is an old anonymous poem. It is a protest against the rich and how they are treated better than the poor.

The Common and the Goose

The law locks up the man or woman
Who steals the goose from off the **common**
But leaves the greater **felon** loose
Who steals the common from the goose

Anonymous

Word bank
common – common land
felon – criminal

In 'The Common and the Goose' there is rhyme at the end of each pair of lines. This is called 'rhyming couplets'. Rhyme like this is very suited to short poems. It has a punchy effect and seems to sum up an idea. All the rhymes are key words.

The poet controls the length of the lines by having exactly the same number of syllables in each line of the couplet. These syllables are organised into a pattern of stressed and unstressed beats.

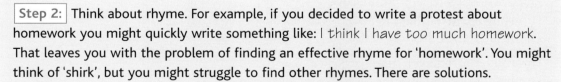

But **leaves** the **grea**ter **fel**on **loose** (four 'beats')

Activity 3 ICT

Write your own short protest poem in rhyming couplets. Make it four lines long so that you use two rhyming couplets. Try to have the same number of syllables in each line.

Step 1: Think of an idea for something you wish to protest about. It doesn't have to be serious.

Step 2: Think about rhyme. For example, if you decided to write a protest about homework you might quickly write something like: I think I have too much homework. That leaves you with the problem of finding an effective rhyme for 'homework'. You might think of 'shirk', but you might struggle to find other rhymes. There are solutions.

◆ Change your line so that it ends with a different word. You might change your line to: I get too much homework from my school.

◆ If you decide it is important to end the line with the key word 'homework', you could use rhyme that isn't perfect. For example, words that end in a 'k' sound, like 'luck' or an 'rk' sound, like 'dark' might give you some ideas.

Step 3: Think about what you have written. When you have worked out your two rhyming couplets, read them aloud and think about the rhythm. Try to work a pattern of beats into your lines.

Developing ideas on poetry

Rhyme and rhythm are patterns. They are based on a sound being repeated. Read the following poem by Adrian Mitchell. As you do so, look for the patterns in it and list them. For example, in the first stanza you'll find the following patterns:

- ◆ Line 2 rhymes with line 4.
- ◆ The last word in every line is a monosyllable.
- ◆ The word 'says' is repeated in every line.
- ◆ The first two lines are both about the same thing (human bodies).
- ◆ The last two lines are about the same thing (weather).

Check to see if these same patterns are repeated in the rest of the poem and if there are any other examples of patterns.

Yes

A smile says: Yes.
A heart says: Blood.
When the rain says: Drink,
The earth says: Mud.

5   The kangaroo says: Trampoline.
Giraffes say: Tree.
A bus says: Us,
While a car says: Me.

Lemon trees say: Lemons.
10 A jug says: Lemonade.
The villain says: You're wonderful.
The hero says: I'm afraid.

The forest says: Hide and Seek.
The grass says: Green and Grow.
15 The railway says: Maybe.
The prison says: No.

The millionaire says: Take.
The beggar says: Give.
The soldier cries: Mother!
20 The baby sings: Live.

The river says: Come with me.
The moon says: Bless.
The stars say: Enjoy the light.
The sun says: Yes.

Adrian Mitchell

Activity 4 (WS)

1 When you have finished reading 'Yes' and thought about the various patterns in it, share your thoughts with a partner. What patterns can you find?

2 Because there are patterns, you notice when there is a change to the pattern. Throughout the poem the poet uses 'say' or 'says', apart from in the penultimate stanza. Discuss with your partner why you think he uses 'cries' (line 19) and 'sings' (line 20)? Look at the following suggestions and decide which you think are best.

   ◆ It simply brings a bit of variety and makes the poem more interesting.
   ◆ It draws attention to this pair of lines because the ideas here are especially important.
   ◆ It emphasises how strongly the poet feels about war and how soldiers die. It helps him to emphasise the importance of life and living.

3 Some of the ideas in the poem are quite straightforward – for example, the idea that lemon trees say 'Lemons' (line 9). But some of the ideas require a little more thought. Copy the chart below. Look again at the lines in column one and discuss their meaning with a partner. A possible explanation is provided for the first one.

The lines	An explanation
A bus says: Us, (line 7) While a car says: Me. (line 8)	The writer is making a point about transport. Large numbers of people can share the same bus. Cars often have only one driver. So it's a lot more selfish to use a car, and worse for the environment.
The railway says: Maybe. (line 15) The prison says: No. (line 16)	
The millionaire says: Take. (line 17) The beggar says: Give. (line 18)	
The soldier cries: Mother! (line 19) The baby sings: Live. (line 20)	
The river says: Come with me. (line 21) The moon says: Bless. (line 22)	

Activity 5 ICT

In his poem on page 78, Adrian Mitchell has used a list structure to put forward a range of ideas. He lists nouns – bus, railway, river – and associates an idea with them. Some are light-hearted, such as the association of kangaroos and trampolines, and some are more serious, such as his ideas on the difference between buses and cars. Use the same structure and approach to write your own poem.

Step 1: Plan the pattern of the stanzas. Make sure you are aware of the following patterns.

A smile says: Yes.	When the rain says: Drink,
A heart says: Blood.	The earth says: Mud.

- ◆ Each stanza contains four lines.
- ◆ The second line always rhymes with the fourth line.
- ◆ Each line is split into two. The first half begins with a phrase and, with a couple of exceptions, uses the verb 'says' or 'say'. Then there is a colon followed by what the thing 'says'. Often it is only one word, but not always.
- ◆ Nearly every line ends with a full stop or a comma. An exclamation mark may be used for emphasis.

Step 2: Brainstorm some ideas. This is the kind of poem you just need to start and see where the form takes you. Choose almost any noun at random – for example, 'teenager'. List a few ideas. Think about days of the week, months, seasons, buildings, places, etc. Different people would think different things. Some might write: 'A teenager says: Future.' Others might write: 'A teenager says: Trouble.'

Step 3: Pair your ideas. Adrian Mitchell pairs, for example, 'rain' and 'earth', and 'millionaire' and 'beggar'. If your poem said: 'A teenager says: Trouble', you might then think of what you could pair with it – for example, 'A grandmother says: Peace.'

Step 4: Think about rhyme. As you pair ideas it is important to think about rhyme. If you had written:

A teenager says: Trouble.
A grandmother says: Peace.

the next thing to consider is what rhymes with 'peace'. The word 'increase' rhymes. So you could add:

Death says: Stop!
But birth says: Increase.

Step 5: Complete your poem. When you have written one four-line stanza, read it to a partner. Ask your partner if it fits the pattern of the original poem (see page 78), and if your ideas are clear. Listen to what your partner says, then decide whether to revise your poem. Write two more stanzas.

Sonnets

There are lots of different structures in poetry. One of the most common is the sonnet. These are usually fourteen-line poems that rhyme in particular patterns.

Read Sonnet 18 slowly, four lines at a time.

Sonnet 18

Shall I compare **thee** to a summer's day?
Thou art more lovely and more **temperate**.
Rough winds do shake the darling buds of May,
And summer's **lease** hath all too short a date.
5 Sometime too hot the eye of heaven shines,
And often is his gold complexion dimmed,
And every fair from **fair** sometimes declines,
By chance, or nature's changing course **untrimmed**.
But **thy eternal** summer shall not fade
10 Nor lose possession of that fair thou **ow'st**,
Nor shall death **brag** thou wander'st in his shade
When in eternal **lines** to time thou grow'st,
So long as men can breathe or eyes can see,
So long lives **this**, and this gives life to thee.

William Shakespeare

Word bank

thee/thou/thy – old forms of you and your
temperate – not extreme; not too hot
lease – a contract that lasts a certain length of time
fair – beauty
untrimmed – having something ornamental removed
eternal – something that lasts for ever
ow'st – own
brag – boast
lines – his poem
this – the poem

Activity 6 ⓦⓢ ⓘⓒⓣ

Summarise each of the four stages of Shakespeare's sonnet using a chart like the one below. The first one has been done for you.

Lines	Rhyme	My summary
1–4	ABAB: day/temperate May/date	In this opening section, Shakespeare asks the question whether the woman he loves is more beautiful than a summer's day. He answers by writing that she's better because the weather in May is sometimes not too good; and because summer doesn't last very long.
5–8		
9–12		
13–14		

Activity 7

Work in pairs to write a sonnet. Your sonnet should be about 'Schooldays' – simply because that is something that virtually everyone has experienced. It is a subject that can easily be broken down into sections. It may help you to organise your answer in the following way.

Step 1: First you need to think about the structure of your ideas. Use a planning chart like the one below.

Lines	Notes
1–4	Could be about Infants/Playschool – carefree, colouring, 'accidents'
5–8	Move on to Juniors – times tables, literacy hour
9–12	Secondary school – moving to a new school, things getting harder
13–14	Sum up school days? Look ahead to next stage?

Step 2: Think about approximate line length. Spend some time trying out some opening lines. Aim for either eight or ten syllables.

Step 3: When you have decided on the number of syllables in a line you should start to work on the rhymes. Work on four lines at a time, remembering the ABAB pattern. You will find that trying to find the rhyme leads to some lines you will be unhappy with, but concentrate on getting a first rough draft written. As you finish four lines show them to another pair: they may be able to offer advice on how to change the wording.

Step 4: Think about making changes. When you have written fourteen lines in rough you should begin to re-read them and think about lines that seem clumsy. To change them you have the same strategies that you used in Activity 3 (see page 77). You can change the line to have a different rhyming word or you can think of other rhyming words that might not be perfect rhymes but are close.

Step 5: Finish your sonnet. When you have done so, discuss the following questions with your partner and agree on responses that you can write down.

◆ Have we successfully broken down our sonnet into four parts?

◆ Does our closing rhyming couplet bring the poem to a satisfactory conclusion?

◆ Are there sections of the poem that rhyme in a way that pleases us?

◆ Are there sections where we know the rhyme is not satisfactory?

Read the following poem. It is about rejection, about being 'stood up' for the first time. The girl in the poem has just phoned someone and what the person said has hurt her.

First Ice

A girl freezes in a telephone booth.
In her draughty overcoat she hides
A face all smeared
In tears and lipstick.

5 She breathes on her thin palms.
Her fingers are icy. She wears earrings.
She'll have to go home alone, alone,
Along the icy street.

First ice. It is the first time.
10 The first ice of telephone phrases.
Frozen tears glitter on her cheeks –
The first ice of human hurt.

Andrei Voznesensky

Write a story entitled 'First Ice' about the experience of being hurt or let down for the first time.

If you wish, you could use the story of the poem. It could be a straightforward story or one told by two narrators.

You might decide to change the focus of the story away from the idea of a date and write about:

◆ a friendship breaking up

◆ the realisation that someone you looked up to wasn't as perfect as you thought

◆ someone whose life has been wonderful until one particular moment when something happened

◆ any other ideas you have.

1 Decide on a story that will suit the title.

2 Plan your story.

3 Write your story. It is especially important that you:

    ◆ give your story a very clear structure   ◆ use a range of sentence styles.

Section C ◆ Reading non-fiction and media texts
Introduction

Non-fiction texts are not poems, stories, novels or plays. They are not made up. There is a huge range of non-fiction texts. They include letters, diaries, leaflets, articles and advertisements. 'The media' is the name given to types of communication that reach large numbers of people, such as television, radio, the Internet and newspapers.

In Year 8 you will have examined a range of non-fiction and media texts, distinguishing between fact, opinion and theory, identifying argument and developing awareness of the author's point of view. You will have considered the importance of presentation and developed your own research skills.

You will be building on these skills in the three units in this section.

In Unit 9, *Thinking about perspectives*, you will examine a range of autobiographical writing. You will consider how authorial techniques and styles vary. You will also identify the perspectives offered on individuals, community and society, and compare the presentation of emotions in related texts.

In Unit 10, *Investigating advertising*, you will identify how meaning is conveyed through print and images. You will consider the link between content, purpose and audience. You will also reflect on the impact advertising has on our lives.

In Unit 11, *Recognising bias*, you will learn how to distinguish between objectivity and bias. You will analyse how a writer can use language to reinforce bias. You will also evaluate the reliability of information available through a media source.

Unit 12 tests you on the skills you will develop as you work carefully through the three units.

9 Thinking about perspectives

This unit will help you to:
- ◆ review and develop your own reading experiences
- ◆ understand how techniques and styles vary
- ◆ use notes for representing information
- ◆ identify the perspectives offered on individuals, community and society
- ◆ compare the presentation of emotions in related texts.

Looking at autobiography

One form of non-fiction is autobiography. An autobiography is an account of a person's life written by that person. List any autobiographies you have read or know of. What kinds of people write autobiographies? Do they have anything in common? Can you recommend any of the autobiographies you have read? If so, which ones and why? Keep a copy of your list.

Finding out about the writer

Autobiographies are often written in chronological order, starting with the writer's childhood. The opening often sets the tone for the whole book. It may reveal details about the kind of person the writer is and the culture in which s/he grew up.

Activity 1 WS

Read the two passages on pages 86 and 87, and make notes on:

- ◆ what the writers are like based on their actions, words, thoughts and the actions of others towards them
- ◆ details about the writers' cultures based on background detail.

You could use a chart like the one below or decide on a different method.

	Chinese Cinderella	*Is That It?*
What I learn about the writer. *(It will help you to think about: age, family, attitude to school, character, behaviour.)*		
What I learn about the culture in which the writer grew up. *(It will help you to think about: country, religion, education, language.)*		

Highlight any significant similarities and differences between the writers and their cultures.

Chinese Cinderella

Autumn, 1941.

p.206

As soon as I got home from school, Aunt Baba noticed the silver medal dangling from the left breast-pocket of my uniform. She was combing her hair in front of the mirror in our room when I rushed in and plopped my school-bag down on my bed.

5   'What's that hanging on your dress?'

'It's something special that Mother Agnes gave me in front of the whole class this afternoon. She called it an award.'

My aunt looked thrilled. 'So soon? You only started kindergarten one week ago. What is it for?'

10   'It's for topping my class this week. When Mother Agnes pinned it on my dress, she said I could wear it for seven days. Here, this certificate goes with it.' I opened my school-bag and handed her an envelope as I climbed on to her lap.

She opened the envelope and took out the certificate.

'Why, it's all written in French or English or some other foreign language. How do
15   you expect me to read this, my precious little treasure?' I knew she was pleased because she was smiling as she hugged me. 'One day soon,' she continued, 'you'll be able to translate all this into Chinese for me. Until then, we'll just write today's date on the envelope and put it away somewhere safe. Go close the door properly and put on the latch so no one will come in.'

20   I watched her open her **closet** door and take out her safe-deposit box. She took the key from a gold chain around her neck and placed my certificate underneath her jade bracelet, pearl necklace and diamond watch – as if my award were also some precious jewel impossible to replace.

As she closed the lid, an old photograph fell out. I picked up the faded picture and
25   saw a solemn young man and woman, both dressed in old-fashioned Chinese robes. The man looked rather familiar.

'Is this a picture of my father and dead mama?' I asked.

'No. This is the wedding picture of your grandparents. Your Ye Ye was twenty-six and your Nai Nai was only fifteen.' She quickly took the photo from me and locked it
30   in her box.

*from **Chinese Cinderella** by Adeline Yen Mah*

Word bank
closet – a cupboard or store room

An hour lasts a lifetime

Frank Lahiffe loved Mary O'Dwyer as well. It was an intolerable triangle. She probably loathed both of us, but, at the age of four, I was not in the least interested in her feelings. The nuns compounded my headache by placing Mary in a desk between Lahiffe and me. Learning my letters, I would trace the 'D' with my finger. It was cut

5 from sandpaper and stuck on light blue cardboard. We would close our eyes and feel the shape of the 'D' while mouthing its sound. 'Duh', I muttered with the others, but my eyes were slits of **guile**, partly open to facilitate my observation of the nun. When she looked away, I darted to the next desk and planted a kiss on Mary's knee. She sat there, eyes clamped tight, now muttering, 'Fuh'.

10 Lahiffe, more absorbed by his rival than his alphabet, then repeated my manoeuvre, kissing la O'Dwyer's other knee. She burst into tears. 'Mary O'Dwyer, stop being a cissy', said the nun, not bothering to enquire into the reasons for the four-year-old's distress. 'Guh', said Lahiffe and I.

Probably I was Robin Hood that day. I could have been Davy Crockett. I had both

15 the outfits made for me by my mother or Auntie Fifi, the dressmaker. However no one could see beneath the brown smocks I and the other boys wore. The girls wore light blue. When it was sunny we had our lessons under the tree in the playground. Lahiffe and I bunked out and went to the shop across the road for sweets. This was forbidden. It was a main road and dangerous for four-year-olds. We were caught

20 sometimes and subjected to a peculiarly cruel form of punishment. We had to stand at the corner till the No. 5 bus had gone before we could walk home. The No. 5 seemed to have no fixed timetable, it appeared wholly at random if it appeared at all. At four or five one was besieged with the psychological terror, not of delayed teatime, but of the possibility that you would have to wait 'all night, if that's how long it takes', or

25 even an hour. I can remember when an hour was a lifetime.

*from **Is That It?** by Bob Geldof*

Word bank
guile – cunning

Activity 2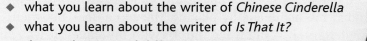

Using your notes from Activity 1 to help you, write about:

◆ what you learn about the writer of *Chinese Cinderella*
◆ what you learn about the writer of *Is That It?*
◆ the similarities and differences between both writers.

Aim to complete your writing in 15 minutes. It will help if you organise it into three paragraphs, based on the list above. Here are some paragraph starters and useful phrases to help you.

First paragraph	In the first extract …	this suggests that …
Second paragraph	The second extract reveals …	making me think that …
		giving the impression that …
Third paragraph	A comparison of the two extracts shows that …	similarly …
		in contrast …
		on the other hand …
		in the same way …

When you have finished, read through what you have written and match it against this checklist.

◆ Have you organised your response into three clear paragraphs?
◆ Are your thoughts expressed clearly so that the reader will understand them?
◆ Look back at your notes. Tick the details you have included. Have you missed out anything that it might be useful to include?
◆ Did you use your time well, perhaps by dividing up the task into three five-minute blocks, one for each paragraph?

Give yourself a grade from A (astonishing) to D (dreadful). Then write a short comment to explain the grade you have awarded.

Writing autobiography in the first person

In both of the autobiography passages you have read, the authors have chosen to write in the first person voice – as the examples below show.

As soon as I got home from school, Aunt Baba noticed the silver medal dangling from the left breast-pocket of my uniform (lines 1–2 of *Chinese Cinderella*).

She probably loathed both of us, but, at the age of four, I was not in the least interested in her feelings (lines 2–4 of *Is That It?*).

Activity 3 ⓦⓢ ⓘⓒⓣ

With a partner, talk about the advantages and disadvantages of using the first person narrative voice. Here are some questions for you to think about.

◆ How does it help you to learn about the writer's thoughts and feelings?
◆ Does it help to make the situation seem real? If so, how?
◆ Does it allow the writer to stand back and judge things objectively?
◆ Does it make the writing more or less personal?

List your points in a chart like the one below. Keep this chart to help you complete Activity 5 (page 91) and Activity 8 (page 93).

Narrative voice	Advantages	Disadvantages
First person voice (Activity 3)		
Second person voice (Activity 5)		
Third person voice (Activity 8)		

Writing autobiography in the second person

While the first person narrative is the most common choice for an autobiography, it is not the only one. In the following extract, Simon Armitage recalls a memorable football match. Unusually, he writes in the second person.

Read the first extract closely, in which the use of the second person is underlined for you.

Word bank
Old Trafford – the football ground where Manchester United play their home games

Subbuteo – a table-top football game where you flick the players with your fingers to pass the ball and score goals

All Points North

You were thirteen when you first went to **Old Trafford**. Being a Town fan, you'd never seen fifty thousand people gathered together in one lump, and you'd certainly never seen European football. You'd never been to a floodlit match either, and the teams came on to the pitch like **Subbuteo** men tipped
5   out on a snooker table. This was in the days before supporting Manchester United became like supporting U2 or the Sony Corporation, in the days when you handed cash over the turnstile and walked on to the terrace.

Activity 4

Talk about the following questions.

1 Who is the 'you' referred to in the passage above?

2 Could it be anyone else?

3 How does the use of the second person in these lines affect you as a reader?

4 What do you think the writer is trying to achieve by using the second person?

Word bank
Juventus – a football team from Italy

Stretford End – the end of the pitch where the fans stand

Now read the second extract from the same book.

United were playing **Juventus**, whose goalie, Dino Zoff, was reckoned to be the best in the world at the time. As he trotted out towards the **Stretford End** where
10   you were standing, a light ripple of applause ran around the ground, and he lifted his arm and held his index finger in the air, to collect the praise and to confirm his status as the world's number one. That was his big mistake. Suddenly he was staring at tens of thousands of outstretched arms, each one carrying a fist or two fingers, and the insults speared at him needed no translation into Italian. Zoff had
15   fallen for the electric handshake. In another sense, in a split second he'd elevated himself from goalkeeper to God, and the crowd were having none of it. For the rest of the match he was a troubled and lonely figure, stood as far away from the crowd as possible, only coming near to pick the ball out of the net.

The writer only uses the second person once in this paragraph.

Having placed the reader firmly in the Stretford End, what does the writer concentrate on next? Why does he not use the second person again?

Finally, read the last extract from this book.

The next round was against **Ajax**, in the days when Ajax was still pronounced like a
20 bathroom cleaner. You were in the **Scoreboard End**. Before the kick-off, a man behind you
leant over the barrier and spat a hot wet blob of bubble gum into your hair. Your friend's
Dad told you to leave it alone, but you messed with it for ninety minutes, and when you got
back, you had to have a bald patch hacked into the top of your head to get rid of the
chuddie. At school next day, you got battered for saying where you'd been, and battered
25 again for looking like a medieval monk. You can't remember the score, but the net outcome
was a defeat.

*from **All Points North** by Simon Armitage*

Word bank
Ajax – a Dutch football team
Scoreboard End – the end of the
pitch where the scoreboard is
chuddie – muck

Activity 5

Talk about the following questions with other students.

1 How many times does the writer use 'you' or 'your' in all three parts of this extract?

2 In what way does the writer move from a general experience in the second
paragraph (lines 8–18) to a very personal one in the third (lines 19–26)?

3 Who is the 'you' in the final paragraph?

4 Re-read the whole extract. What are the advantages and disadvantages of writing
autobiography in the second person?

Add your points to the chart you began in Activity 3 on page 89.

Aspects of culture

You will probably have come across the term 'culture' when discussing writers whose cultures differ from yours. However, the word has many other associations. Look at the illustrations on this page. You could make your own notes on the term 'culture' using these ideas and others of your own.

Activity 6 ICT

Writers of autobiography often comment on aspects of their own culture. Read the following sentence closely, which comes from the passage on page 90, and think about the underlined words and phrases:

This was in the days before supporting Manchester United became like supporting U2 or the Sony Corporation, in the days when you handed cash over the turnstile and walked on to the terrace (lines 5–7).

1 For each word or phrase try to work out what the author is really saying. The first one, 'like supporting U2', has been done for you.

> U2: Major band of the last 20 years. Members glamorous and hugely wealthy. Set trends and appear on television and in magazines. Footballers are being compared to pop stars and the team to a band.

2 What word would you use to describe the tone of this sentence? Would it be 'serious', 'funny', 'sarcastic', 'ironic', 'witty' or something else? Give a reason for your choice.

3 Put your ideas together to explain what the author is implying about football today.

Identifying use of humour

In autobiography, as in other forms of writing, authors often use humour to entertain the reader. Even if you don't find it funny, you need to be able to identify and comment on a writer's use of humour.

Activity 7

In this activity you will need to decide how you and a partner can best record your research in order to report back to another pair. Before you start, read through the task carefully and decide:

◆ how much detail you need to record
◆ what form your notes should take.

1 Re-read the passages from *Is That It?* (see page 87) and *All Points North* (see pages 90–91). With a partner identify examples of humour in each extract. Decide whether the humour comes from:

   ◆ the incident described
   ◆ the words used to describe it
   ◆ both of the above
   ◆ something else.

2 Now join another pair. Take it in turns to explain how you think the humour is created in each of the passages.

The writer's stance

It is important to recognise the stance or position taken by a writer. So far you have read autobiographical extracts written in the voice of the first and second person. In her autobiography, written in the third person, Flora Thompson writes about life in a small Oxfordshire hamlet in the late nineteenth century. In the extract on page 94 she describes a typical meal.

Activity 8 (WS)

1 As you read the passage from *Lark Rise to Candleford*, think about:
   a the different effects of the use of the third person
   b advantages of writing in the third person.

2 Add your points to the chart you began in Activity 3 on page 89.

A good dinner

Here, then, were the three chief ingredients of the one hot meal a day, bacon from the **flitch**, vegetables from the garden, and flour for the roly-poly. This meal, called 'tea', was taken in the evening, when the men were home from the fields and the children from school, for neither could get home at midday.

5   About four o'clock, smoke would go up from the chimneys, as the fire was made up and the big iron boiler, or the three-legged pot, was slung on the hook of the chimney-chain. Everything was cooked in the one utensil; the square of bacon, amounting to little more than a taste each; cabbage, or other green vegetables in one net, potatoes in another, and the roly-poly swathed in a cloth. It sounds a haphazard method in these

10 days of gas and electric cookers; but it answered its purpose, for, by carefully timing the putting in of each item and keeping the simmering of the pot well regulated, each item was kept intact and an appetising meal was produced. The water in which the food had been cooked, the potato **parings**, and other vegetable trimmings were the pig's share.

15 When the men came home from work they would find the table spread with a clean whitey-brown cloth, upon which would be knives and two-pronged steel forks with buckhorn handles. The vegetables would then be turned out into big round yellow crockery dishes and the bacon cut into dice, with much the largest cube upon Feyther's plate, and the whole family would sit down to the chief

20 meal of the day. True, it was seldom that all could find places at the central table; but some of the smaller children could sit upon stools with the seat of a chair for a table, or on the doorstep with their plates on their laps.

Good manners prevailed. The children were given their share of the food, there was no picking and choosing, and they were expected to eat it in silence. 'Please'

25 and 'Thank you' were permitted, but nothing more. Father and Mother might talk if they wanted to; but usually they were content to concentrate upon their enjoyment of the meal. Father might shovel green peas into his mouth with his knife, Mother might drink her tea from her saucer, and some of the children might lick their plates when the food was devoured; but who could eat peas with a two-pronged fork, or wait for tea to cool

30 after the heat and flurry of cooking, and licking the plates passed as a graceful compliment to Mother's good dinner. 'Thank God for my good dinner. Thank Father and Mother. Amen' was the grace used in one family, and it certainly had the merit of giving credit where credit was due.

*from **Lark Rise to Candleford** by Flora Thompson*

Word bank
flitch – a side of pork salted and cured
parings – peelings

Activity 9 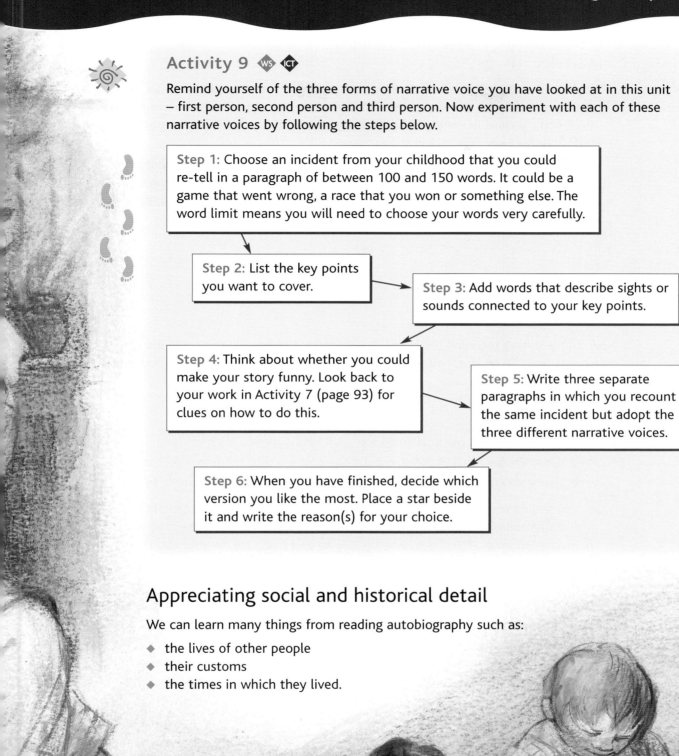 ⓦⓢ ⓘⓒⓣ

Remind yourself of the three forms of narrative voice you have looked at in this unit – first person, second person and third person. Now experiment with each of these narrative voices by following the steps below.

Step 1: Choose an incident from your childhood that you could re-tell in a paragraph of between 100 and 150 words. It could be a game that went wrong, a race that you won or something else. The word limit means you will need to choose your words very carefully.

Step 2: List the key points you want to cover.

Step 3: Add words that describe sights or sounds connected to your key points.

Step 4: Think about whether you could make your story funny. Look back to your work in Activity 7 (page 93) for clues on how to do this.

Step 5: Write three separate paragraphs in which you recount the same incident but adopt the three different narrative voices.

Step 6: When you have finished, decide which version you like the most. Place a star beside it and write the reason(s) for your choice.

Appreciating social and historical detail

We can learn many things from reading autobiography such as:

◆ the lives of other people
◆ their customs
◆ the times in which they lived.

Activity 10 (WS)

Look back at the extract from *Lark Rise to Candleford* (see page 94). In order to create the scene vividly for the reader the writer gives us a wealth of detail relating to the meal. Make a chart like the one below. Then identify the detail from the passage by making notes under the different headings.

Content of the meal	How the meal was prepared	How the table was organised	Behaviour at the table

Now that you have recorded the detail, it is important to be able to assess and make comments on it. To do this, you need to draw on your own experience and knowledge.

Activity 11 (WS)

1 Think of what you consider to be a typical family meal of today.
   a Describe the meal in detail, using a chart identical to the one shown in Activity 10.
   b Think about the similarities and differences between the two meals as you do this.

2 You should now be able to comment on what the passage from *Lark Rise to Candleford* tells you about life in the late nineteenth century compared with life in modern times. You should also be able to give evidence for your comments.
   Use the information you have gathered to organise your ideas into another chart like the one below. This has been started for you.

Comment on life in the 1880s as compared to modern times	Evidence
Limited range of food	Bacon, vegetables and flour were main ingredients
Primitive forms of cooking	

Thinking about how emotions are explored and portrayed

Writers will sometimes touch on sensitive and emotional memories. In the following extract from *Is That It?*, Bob Geldof recalls his mother who died suddenly when he was a small child.

Lipstick, gloves and sequins

Ma was a tall woman who will forever for me wear long black gloves up to her elbows. On the night of the commercial travellers' ball she and my father would come into my room and cuddle me. Even now as I write this there's a sense of unbearable loss. They would have party hats on and the next morning we would wear them. Long black gloves wrapped round me,
5   sequins from her dress sticking sideways into my cheeks. I curled her hair round and round my fingers. It was springy and my finger would go through the empty hollow of the curl. In my other hand, pressed to my nose, would be a ragged piece of cardigan that lulled me to sleep. I imagine the perfume but I remember the lipstick on her teeth. I remember her applying the lipstick and moving close to the mirror. She would press her lips together, sucking
10 them back behind her teeth and rolling them sideways to get an even distribution of the rouge. There would be lipstick on the tea cups. Lipstick, gloves and sequins: not a bad memory of your mother. Later, visiting her grave, we would kneel on the ground and the tiny pieces of stone cut into my knee leaving the same mark as the sequins had on my cheek.

*from **Is That It?** by Bob Geldof*

Activity 12 ⓦ

1   The following comments show some of the methods Geldof uses to convey his feelings about his mother. Re-read the extract closely and match the comments to the appropriate parts of the text. If you have a separate copy of the text you can annotate it by highlighting the appropriate part and writing the comment next to it in the margin. The comments are in the order in which they apply to the text.

> Movement in tenses to link the past, the present and the future.
> How he explains her movements to create a picture.
> Simplicity of expression capturing great pain.
> Uses the adult tone.
> Gives details of the things he remembers.
> Creates a picture of himself as a young child.
> Uses the present tense to make these memories more immediate.
> Uses the second person to create a sense of distance and involve the reader.
> Uses a single connective to link her life to her death.
> Uses the sequins as a symbol of the pain he feels.

2   Talk about how Geldof gets his feelings across to the reader. Focus on these questions.
   a   Does he make any direct reference to his feelings as a child?
   b   How do you know what his feelings were and are?
   c   How do the details he recalls help the reader to understand his feelings?
   d   Why do you think he chose to describe the loss of his mother in this way?

Geldof conveys the pain of his mother's death indirectly through the detail of his description.

In the following extract, Penelope Lively recalls the occasion of her parents' divorce when she was a young girl in Egypt.

Activity 13

1 Read the extract closely with a partner.

  a How does the writer get across the importance of the incident she is describing?

  b What methods does she use to do this? It will help you to think about:

    ◆ the use of different tenses and the reasons for this

    ◆ direct and indirect references to feelings

    ◆ the importance of Tutankhamun's tomb

    ◆ how she creates a picture of herself as a child

    ◆ the links she makes to the future.

2 Decide which features should be annotated and what you want to say about them.

3 Join with another pair. Compare and explain the annotations you have made. If there are any you wish to add or delete from your copy, do so.

Oleander Jacaranda

p.206

I have been taken out for the afternoon by a friend of my father's, a man I have never met before, who has come from Khartoum, where my father is now working. He has taken me to the museum. We look at the things from Tutankhamun's tomb. He explains them to me, in a grown-up way, as though I were older than I am. I stand looking at the great gold mask, at the
5 chariot, at the **sarcophagus**, and am filled with a confused solemnity. Lucy is not with us. I am alone with this stranger whose name and face have subsequently faded away but who hangs over the afternoon as a kindly presence, concerned about me in a way that I cannot identify. I sense his concern, and the fact that I am spotlit in some way, affected as though ill, and that this man is like a doctor, perturbed about an ailment of which I do not feel the symptoms.

10   Lucy is not with us because my parents are getting divorced, and this is the afternoon of the court hearing, at which her presence is required. All this has been explained to me, partly by Lucy and partly by my mother. I know too that Lucy and I are going soon to England, for ever, and that I will live first with my grandmothers – going from one to the other – and then later
15 with my father, when he comes from Khartoum.

    I know all this, but passively. I do not know what to do with these facts. They hang above the glass cases in the museum, above the mask, above the jewellery, which are more immediate. I know only that things are out of the ordinary, and that I feel solemn, and vaguely important.

20   I was eleven. Lucy had to be at the court hearing to give evidence as to my mother's adultery. My mother had been living for some while with a man she had met a year or so before – an army officer – and my father had agreed to a divorce. He would be granted custody of me, which my mother

had not requested. Lucy would take me back to England, where my father would find us
25 a home and me a boarding school as soon as he could wind up his affairs in the Sudan.

Back then, divorce was not the commonplace happening that it is today. It carried a
stigma. I had heard the word – as one uttered by grown-ups in a particular tone, a
mysteriously loaded word. Lucy and I had been living for some while cheek by jowl with
my mother's new domestic arrangements, and were offended by them. Our reaction had
30 been to withdraw into our private **enclave**. We tried to ignore my mother and her
companion, and they steered clear of us.

Thinking about it all now, I see that I was in a sense cushioned from the effect of
divorce by the distance that there had always been between my mother and myself. The
fact that she was now, in effect, discarding me along with my father was not as
35 shattering as it would be for a child for whom a mother is the crucial figure. I would still
have Lucy, who was far more important to me. It would be Lucy who would take me to
England. It never occurred to me that I would have to lose Lucy also, eventually. And in
the event I was not to see my mother again for two years, after we left Egypt, by which
time I was someone else.
40 I do not know who the kindly friend of my father's was who took me to the museum
that day, but my father subsequently wrote to Lucy that he had reported of that
afternoon that I was charming and very nicely behaved. I was much **gratified** by this;
nobody had ever said such a thing before.
And when, years later, I saw the Tutankhamun
45 treasures again, the immediacies were
reversed: the mask and the chariot sank away
and the **portentous** atmosphere of that
afternoon came flooding back.

*from **Oleander Jacaranda** by Penelope Lively*

Word bank

sarcophagus – a stone coffin
stigma – a mark of disgrace
enclave – an enclosure surrounded by foreign territory
gratified – pleased
portentous – indicating that something momentous
is going to happen

Activity 14

In this passage, Penelope Lively gives the reader a range of viewpoints on the subject
of divorce.
What do we learn about the views of the following on divorce?
◆ The writer as a child. ◆ The society in which she lived. ◆ The writer as an adult.

Activity 15

Look back at the list of autobiographies you made at the start of this unit (see
page 85). Add to it the titles and authors of the five autobiographies named in this unit.

1 Which autobiography would you be most interested in reading all the way through?
Why?

2 Place the five in order of preference and aim to read at least one of these within the
next month.

This unit will help you to:
- ◆ recognise the link between content, purpose and audience
- ◆ identify how meaning is conveyed through print and images
- ◆ think about how media texts influence and are influenced by readers
- ◆ compare the use of the same text in different media.

The media and advertising

As you will know, 'the media' is the general term given to the different forms of mass communication such as television, radio, cinema, the Internet, newspapers and magazines. These are the forms of communication that reach large numbers of people in a relatively short time. Advertising has a significant role in the media.

Activity 1 ⓦⓢ

Read the following advertisements, then copy and complete the chart by identifying:
- ◆ the main features of each advert
- ◆ where you might find them.

The first one has been done for you.

Text	Main features of advert	Where you might find it
A	Short, informative, factual and to the point.	'For Sale' section of a local newspaper.

A

SONY D-191
Discman, digital
volume, earphones,
AC power adaptor,
silver, slim design,
perfect working
order **£80**
Tel 0875 724391

B

Spot
check

When it comes to beating spots, acne or other skin problems, creams or sticks only touch the surface. The secret of a healthy, spotless complexion goes deeper than that.

Clear Complexion tablets contain natural active herbs that help to treat your skin from within. So your skin stays clear of spots - even under close inspection! Available from Boots, Superdrug, large Tesco and Asda stores, Holland and Barrett, health shops and pharmacies.

Jessup Marketing, London WC1N 3XX.
www.jessup.co.uk

C

for sale

for sale

D

WDCS
reg charity no: 1014705

The global voice for
the protection of
whales, dolphins
and their
environment

working on campaigns &
projects in over 25 countries

Linking content to purpose and audience

When designing an advertisement, advertisers have a specific purpose in mind. It could be that they want to:

◆ sell a product or a lifestyle
◆ remind the reader of a particular brand name – this is often referred to as 'raising brand awareness'
◆ persuade the reader to act or think in a particular way.

Think of, and list, examples of advertisements that match each of these categories.

When designing an advertisement, advertisers have a specific audience in mind. This audience is usually defined by:

◆ gender ◆ age
◆ interests ◆ needs.

The audience of an advert is often referred to as the consumer. Adverts can have more than one purpose and more than one audience. Generally, the content contains clues that help you to identify the purpose(s) and the audience(s). Look back to text A. The purpose of this advert is to sell the Discman by informing the reader of its qualities.

Activity 2 WS

Copy the chart below, then complete it by identifying the purpose(s) and audience(s) of the adverts on page 100. The first one has been done for you.

Text	Purpose(s)	Audience(s)
A	To sell the Discman. To inform the reader of its qualities.	Readers of the newspaper with an interest in music.

Presentation and its effect

One of the first things advertisers need to consider is how to present their material. They need to attract and keep their audience's attention as well as get a particular message across. The visual impact of the advert can be very important. When assessing visual impact you need to consider:

◆ first impressions
◆ use of illustrations and different fonts
◆ use of colour
◆ layout.

Look at and read the following tour advertisement carefully. As you do, note your answers to the questions that surround the advertisement. Your notes are for your use, to help you assess the presentation. You can abbreviate and do not need to write in sentences.

What do you first notice when you look at the advertisement?

Choose one word to sum up your first impression.

What are you shown in the pictures?

What is suggested by the cartoon frog?

What use is made of different fonts?

Why might the London Tourist Board logo be included?

Where does the word 'unique' appear and what does it suggest?

Where does the word 'adventure' appear and what does it suggest?

How is the material organised?

What is unusual about the shape?

Why is there a prominence of blue?

What can you say about the use of colour?

Activity 3 (WS) (ICT)

Use the notes that you made about the Frog Tours advert opposite to help you answer the following question:

> *How does the presentation of the Frog Tours advertisement target its purpose and audience?*

Read through all the steps of how to answer this question before starting to write.

Step 1: Organise your ideas into two paragraphs:

◆ one dealing with intended purpose(s)
◆ one dealing with intended audience(s).

Step 2: Colour-code your notes to show the details you want to include in each paragraph.

Step 3: Before you start to write, read these opening sentences. The annotations highlight the features of the writing for you. You can use these sentences as the opening to your answer.

Opens with a statement, making clear what the paragraph is about.

Uses a formal tone.

The Frog Tours advertisement [has] a number of different purposes. The first of these [is] to attract attention and [in order to do this] it uses bright, vibrant colours.
It also ...

Written in the present tense.

Refers to features and/or details of the text to support points.

Step 4: Remember to connect your ideas clearly and logically. Here are some useful connecting words and phrases:

◆ secondly ...
◆ furthermore ...
◆ additionally ...

◆ this suggests that ...
◆ this implies ...
◆ however ...

◆ seems to be ...
◆ creates an impression of ...
◆ so as to ...

Examining words in detail

Advertisers often use language in unusual ways in order to create particular effects.
Look at this phrase:

New power in action!

What does it mean? What does it suggest? What is the purpose of the exclamation mark? What kind of product might this phrase be used to advertise? Talk about the different possibilities. Now turn the page.

Activity 4 (WS) (ICT)

In this activity you will look closely at the way language is used in the beyerdynamic advert.

1 Examine and talk about each of the words and phrases in the first column before copying and completing the chart. The first two lines have been filled in for you.

Words/ phrases	The impressions the words give	Things associated with the words	Things suggested by the words
beyerdynamic	Powerful, hard-hitting	Dynamo, dynamic, dynamite	Energy, power, movement
Powerful	Strong equipment	Power (repeated from dynamo)	Powerful compared to others
The world leader			
Microphones destined to perform for you			
A powerful performance every time!			
Audition Opus today			
What real power is about			
Fidelity in Audio			

2 How many times do the following words appear in this advert?

◆ 'power' or 'powerful' ◆ 'perform' or 'performance' ◆ 'beyerdynamic'

What is the effect of this repetition?

3 Using the information in your chart and your answers to question 2, what comments can you now make about the ways language is used to create particular effects? List them as separate points.

Examining images in detail

Advertisers give as much thought to their choice of images as they do to their choice of words. A useful way to explore the use of images is to ask a series of questions, like the ones opposite.

What do the pictures show?

What is suggested by each picture?

What associations do the pictures have?

Which image has most impact?

How do the images link with purpose and audience?

How are they placed in relation to each other and the printed text?

What colours are used? What effect do they have?

Activity 5 ICT

1 Talk through the questions on page 105 in relation to the pictures in the beyerdynamic advert on page 104. Make a note of your answers.

2 Use your notes to help you write a paragraph of approximately eight to ten sentences explaining how images are used in the beyerdynamic advert. Remember to:
   - ◆ write in the present tense
   - ◆ use a formal tone
   - ◆ use a range of connectives such as 'therefore', 'consequently', 'alternatively' and 'so'
   - ◆ re-read your explanation to check it is clear.

Responding to advertising

Advertising affects people. It influences what they buy, how they think, who they vote for and which charities they support. It is because advertising works that companies are prepared to put huge amounts of money into it on a regular basis. If it didn't work, they wouldn't bother. Advertisers feed off our:

   - ◆ fears   ◆ insecurities   ◆ desires   ◆ sympathies   ◆ senses.

They aim to make us feel something so that we take notice and read on.

WATCH OUT! There's a thief about!

Having a BAD HAIR DAY?

This tiny kitten was brutally beaten and left to die.

YOU TOO CAN BE A MILLIONAIRE!

Taste the fruity flavour.

How the media is influenced

Just as advertising influences the reader, so the reader can influence the content of the advertisement. In the following extract from its website, Barnardo's, a children's charity, explains the thinking behind its new campaign.

Activity 6

1 As you read the extract from the Barnardo's website, identify:
   a the reasons it wants to change its image
   b the ways in which it is trying to change its image.

2 The Barnardo's campaign is described as 'hard-hitting' and not a 'soft sell'.
   a Think about what these two terms mean. Write your own definition of each term and check it against a partner's.
   b Talk about how you could apply these terms to other adverts you know.

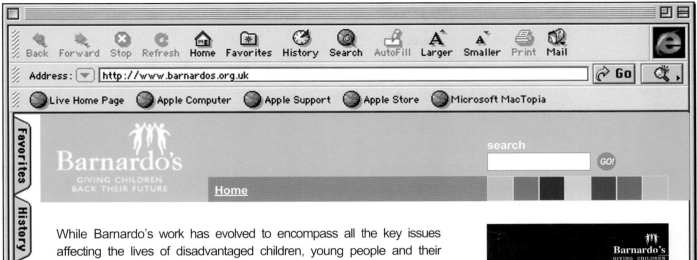

Back   Forward   Stop   Refresh   Home   Favorites   History   Search   AutoFill   Larger   Smaller   Print   Mail

Address: http://www.barnardos.org.uk   Go

Live Home Page   Apple Computer   Apple Support   Apple Store   Microsoft MacTopia

Barnardo's
GIVING CHILDREN
BACK THEIR FUTURE

search   GO!

Home

While Barnardo's work has evolved to encompass all the key issues affecting the lives of disadvantaged children, young people and their families, the public image of the organisation has not kept pace with this development.

Research shows that the majority of people in the UK retain an essentially historical view of Barnardo's. They continue to see it as a charity running 'orphanages', or large-scale residential childcare facilities. The image of the organisation remains rooted in its past, epitomised by the 'cottage collecting boxes' once a feature of millions of homes.

'Barnardo's has always been about supporting children and young people threatened by poverty, abuse and disadvantage and helping them to reach their potential – that has not changed,' said Roger Singleton. 'The vital challenge now facing the organisation is how to communicate its relevance and deservedness to new generations of potential supporters.'

Barnardo's current communications campaign challenges out-dated views of Britain's biggest children's charity. It positions the organisation in the forefront of the fight to build better futures for disadvantaged, abused and troubled children.

The campaign was led off with a series of advertisements depicting children in a variety of 'adult' situations: homelessness, alcohol and drug abuse, suicide and prison. Though the advertisements are hard-hitting, the message is one of hope – that Barnardo's can help children overcome deprivation and avoid futures like these.

Linked with the advertising campaign are the website and a video designed to engage and inform those who have lost track of what Barnardo's does. The video features case histories of young people involved with the charity's projects. This is not a 'soft sell'; it tackles the challenging and topical issues of teenage pregnancy and child sexual abuse.

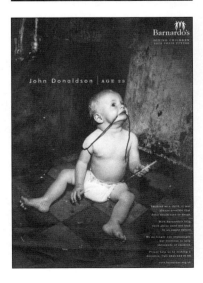

*from the **Barnardo's** website*

Using the same text in different media

Websites often carry advertising material as shown in the Barnardo's example on page 107. Think about the ways advertising on a website is similar to and/or different from advertising in a magazine or newspaper. Working with a partner, map your thoughts on this. Here are some prompts to get you started.

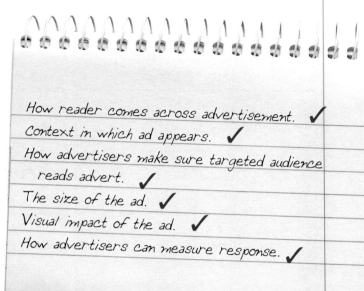

How reader comes across advertisement. ✓

Context in which ad appears. ✓

How advertisers make sure targeted audience reads advert. ✓

The size of the ad. ✓

Visual impact of the ad. ✓

How advertisers can measure response. ✓

Now compare the advertisement captions on the opposite page with the corresponding copy on page 107. Add to your map of similarities and differences.

Writing about advertisements

When you read advertisements you are reading images as well as print. You need to interpret both. Usually you will be asked to write about the content of an advertisement and to comment on its effectiveness.

It is often helpful to have a structure for writing about advertisements. Here is an outline you could use. Remember, not all of it will apply to all advertisements.

Activity 7 ⓦ

Carefully look at, and read, the Barnardo's advert opposite. Spend fifteen minutes making notes as you work through Steps 1 to 6.

Step 1: Describe what you see and your first impressions.

Step 2: Refer to the probable intended purpose and audience.

Step 3: Analyse specific features of the presentation – for example, the background and foreground detail, use of colour and so on.

Step 4: Discuss the link between the print and the image.

Step 5: Comment on interesting uses of language.

Step 6: Evaluate the overall relevance and effectiveness of the advertisement.

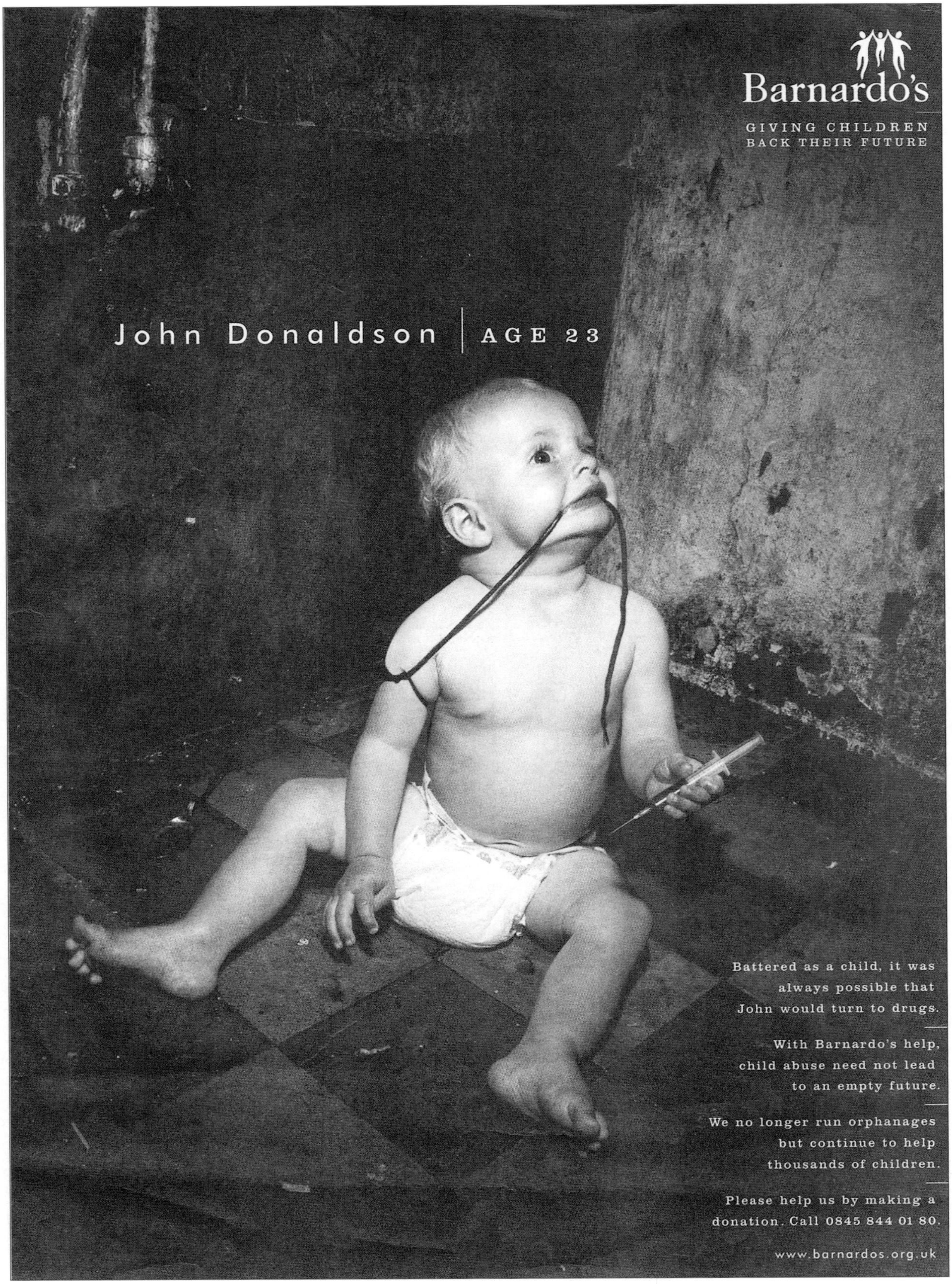
Barnardo's
GIVING CHILDREN
BACK THEIR FUTURE
John Donaldson | AGE 23
Battered as a child, it was
always possible that
John would turn to drugs.
With Barnardo's help,
child abuse need not lead
to an empty future.
We no longer run orphanages
but continue to help
thousands of children.
Please help us by making a
donation. Call 0845 844 01 80.
www.barnardos.org.uk

Activity 8 ICT

Using your notes to help you, write about:

a the ways the ideas are presented in the Barnardo's advert

b the effectiveness of the advert.

Remember to:

◆ write in the present tense

◆ support the points you make with references to the text.

You will be expected to mention:

◆ your first impressions

◆ the targeted purpose and audience

◆ presentational devices

◆ the link between the print and the image

◆ interesting uses of language

◆ how well you think it works and why.

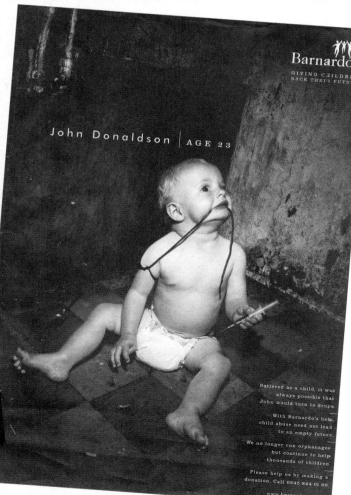

This unit will help you to:

◆ **distinguish between objectivity and bias**

◆ **recognise layers of meaning in the writer's choice of words**

◆ **analyse how a writer can use language to reinforce bias**

◆ **evaluate the reliability of information available through a media source.**

Identifying bias and objectivity

The following three people have different views about the same school. As you read what they say, decide which is the most balanced and fair view of the school. Explain your choice to a partner.

Mr Johnston

Well it's the most popular school in the area and all the parents want their children to go there. You have to put your child's name on a list and they don't all get accepted. Both of mine came here and they did very well. The exam results are always good and they have excellent sport and drama facilities. You can tell the pupils are happy just by looking at them. It's obvious they enjoy going to school and there's never any problems with bullying or anything like that.

Amandeep

I'm very keen on sport, so when I first came to look round here I really liked the look of the sports facilities. The sports field is huge and the indoor gym is very well equipped. Sport aside, we generally get quite a good education here, though some subjects are better than others. I think some of the teachers are too strict. In some lessons we have to sit in boy/girl order when I'd much rather sit with my friends. It's supposed to help you work and, to be fair, not many people misbehave in those lessons.

Tina

My dad was really keen for me to come to this school because he used to, but I wish I'd gone to a different one with my friends. If my parents would let me move to another one I'd go tomorrow. You never learn anything here. All the teachers want you to do is sit in straight rows and be quiet, while they get on with their marking. They're really strict and won't even let you sit next to your friends. They always pick on me and send me out of the class or give me extra work. It's not fair. They never pick on anyone else.

You will have noticed that Mr Johnston and Tina both give unbalanced views. Mr Johnston gives the impression that everything is wonderful and Tina talks as though everything is terrible. Both of them are biased. They are letting their feelings influence their judgement. Amandeep, on the other hand, starts to weigh up the good and bad points. He is not letting his feelings influence his judgement. He is being objective.

Activity 1

1 Add another paragraph to the words of Mr Johnston, Amandeep and Tina. You should aim to keep either the bias or the objectivity.

2 Work in pairs to review the appropriateness of your writing. Read your paragraphs aloud and ask your partner to:
   a identify which person is speaking in each
   b say why they think this.

Developing your understanding of bias

Bias is often shown in people's opinions, as you have seen in the examples on page 111. Bias can also seem to be based on facts. The bias is created by the way the facts are selected and used.

Read this fact file on Samantha Jones.

NAME: Samantha Jones

AGE: 34

FAMILY: husband, Lee; two children, Lisa (5) and Katy (2)

EDUCATION: to GCSE level (French D, English C, Maths C, Geography C, Science D, Food Technology C)

EMPLOYMENT: three mornings and two evenings a week as aerobics instructor at the local leisure centre

INTERESTS: keeping fit, singing with a local choir, going dancing with friends

HOME: three-bedroom first-floor flat in Manor Park Lane

Here are two descriptions of Samantha, based on the fact file. As you read them talk about:

◆ what impression each one gives of Samantha
◆ which is positive and which is negative
◆ which facts have been selected
◆ how the same facts can be used in different ways to create bias.

Description 1

Mother of two, Sammy Jones, likes nothing better than to go dancing with her 'friends' on a Saturday night. Fitness freak Sammy, who left school with a GCSE in Cookery, likes to keep in trim shape for her nights on the town. When she's not out dancing she's doing the aerobics classes at the local leisure centre. Meanwhile little Lisa (5) can only sadly wave goodbye as her mother cheerfully leaves her in their first-floor flat with her baby sister Katy, aged 2.

Description 2

Samantha Jones was keen to return to work once her children, Lisa (5) and Katy (2), were old enough to be looked after by their dad, Lee. Samantha, who lives in a spacious apartment in Manor Park Lane, left school with a string of GCSEs. Always keen to promote the benefits of a healthy lifestyle, she trained as an aerobics instructor and has recently joined the highly qualified staff at the Leisure Centre. When she's not keeping fit our Mum of the Month is singing her heart out with the local church choir.

Activity 2

1 Read this fact file.

Name: Nicholas James Smith

Age: 16

Family: dad Mike, and sister Beth, aged 11

Education: studying for GCSEs at Carlton College Comprehensive School

Employment: part-time Saturdays and Wednesday evenings at the local supermarket

Interests: playing drums with local band, football, girlfriend Lucy

Home: three-bedroom semi in Howton Rd

2 Using only the facts given, write two accounts of Nicholas Smith – one showing positive bias and one showing negative bias. You could record your ideas on a chart like this.

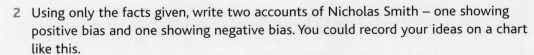

Positive	Fact	Negative
Use 'Nick Smith' to sound friendly	Nicholas James Smith	Use 'Nicholas James Smith' to sound stuffy and dull
Fast approaching adulthood	Age 16	Turbulent teenage years

Identifying bias in language

Newspapers often claim to be objective in their reporting but a close examination of headlines shows this is not always so. Read this headline:

MAD WORLD WHERE CELEBS CASH IN

The use of the word 'mad' suggests foolishness and insanity. 'Cash' suggests something to do with money. When combined with 'in' to make 'cash in' you have a slang term meaning 'to take advantage of'. By using 'mad' and 'cash in' the writer shows he doesn't approve of the amount of money celebrities are getting. He is trying to influence the way the reader thinks before s/he reads the article.

Activity 3

Read the headlines numbered 1 to 3 below, in which the writers make their views clear to the reader by their choice of words. For each one identify:

◆ what point of view is suggested by the headline
◆ which word(s) show(s) the point of view
◆ how these words show the point of view.

An example has been done for you.

This shows me that the writer thinks this is very bad – a disgrace.

This word suggests something very sad and upsetting.

BABY SCANDAL OF HEARTBREAK HOMES

Home is a place where you should feel happy and safe. This is why the link between heartbreak and homes is an unexpected one.

1 # Frail and elderly suffer in a sick society

2 ## BOYS IN CRISIS NOW

3 ## Super Soccer Star Scores Again

Examining bias in images

Bias is found not only in newspaper headlines but also in reports and articles. Look at these photographs.

Photograph A

Photograph B

Activity 4

1 Talk about and make notes on the impressions created of the two men by the:

   ◆ angle and distance at which the photographs have been taken
   ◆ men's facial expressions   ◆ clothes they are wearing   ◆ background details.

Now read these descriptions.

NAME:	Andrew Bennett
AGE:	59
STATUS:	Member of Parliament and former teacher
HOME:	Semi-detached house in Heaton Mersey
INCOME:	£43,000
MANNER:	Concerned intellectual
HOBBIES:	Rambling

NAME:	Nicholas van Hoogstraten
AGE:	53
STATUS:	Landowner and property magnate
HOME:	Building Britain's biggest private house
INCOME:	Unknown, estate valued at £200m
MANNER:	Arrogant in the extreme
HOBBIES:	Wealth

2 Which description would you match to:

   ◆ photograph A?   ◆ photograph B?

   Talk about the reasons for your choice.

3 The writer presents the above descriptions as fact files. Is she right to do so? Analyse them closely. Decide:

   a which details are factual
   b what these facts focus on
   c what impression these facts give the readers
   d how the selection of different facts might have given a different impression
   e how these 'facts' show bias.

Thinking about negative and positive bias

As you have seen, bias can be negative or positive and can be used to influence the reader into supporting a particular idea or point of view. On the next page you will find the full article from which the pictures and fact files on page 115 were taken.

Activity 5 WS ICT

1 Work with a partner. Read the article opposite, noting any examples of negative or positive bias that you come across. Use a chart like the one below.

Negative bias	Positive bias
wealthy landlords	the right to roam
set loose the dogs	basic rights

2 What point of view does the writer put forward about the right to ramble? Use the evidence you have collected to help you discuss this question with a partner.

3 Write a paragraph of no more than 100 words in which you clearly identify the writer's point of view. You should write formally and include evidence to support your ideas.

You could start with:

> The writer seems to think that …

Other useful sentence openers are:

> This suggests that she …   However, it is possible that …

Activity 6 WS

1 Scan the article opposite to identify the additional details you are given about Andrew Bennett and Nicholas van Hoogstraten. Make a chart like the one below and list the details.

Andrew Bennett	Nicholas van Hoogstraten

2 What is each man quoted as saying?

3 Look at your answers to 1 and 2. What do these details tell you about:
   a the way the writer views both men
   b the impression she wants to give the reader?

RUMBLE IN THE COUNTRYSIDE

As walkers and landlords prepare to do battle **Joanne Murphy** looks at life from both sides of the fence

For decades they have been two irreconcilable forces – ramblers who believe they have the right to roam and wealthy landlords who firmly believe they do not.

The two cultures are principles apart. In pursuit of their perception of basic rights, the ramblers have staged much-celebrated mass trespasses and the landlords in return have set loose the dogs and sought remedies in the courts.

The bitterness and the great social divide have rarely been better brought to life than in the amazing conflict involving one of Stockport's MPs and one of the country's richest men.

A noble protector of Britain's humble public footpaths has thrown down the gauntlet to the man who has attempted to bulldoze over them.

In the red corner stands Andrew Bennett, Labour MP for Reddish, and President of the Ramblers Association.

In the true blue corner is Nicholas van Hoogstraten. Multi-millionaire property owner. The man who refers to ramblers in frightening Nazi-speak as "the great unwashed". He is not a man to forgive those who trespass against him.

The battle commenced last week when Andrew Bennett, a lifelong and committed rambler, led a demonstration at van Hoogstraten's High Cross estate in East Sussex. The property tycoon and former slum landlord has blocked an ancient footpath

THE RAMBLER v THE LAND OWNER

NAME: Andrew Bennett
AGE: 59.
STATUS: Member of Parliament and former teacher.
HOME: Semi detached house in Heaton Mersey.
INCOME: £43,000
MANNER: Concerned intellectual.
HOBBIES: Rambling.

NAME: Nicholas van Hoogstraten
AGE: 53.
STATUS: Landowner and property magnate.
HOME: Building Britain's biggest private house – £30m of it.
INCOME: Unknown, estate valued at £200m.
MANNER: Arrogant in the extreme.
HOBBIES: Wealth.

which runs through his land. He says he wants to keep the so-called unwashed out.

Two more contrasting men there could not be.

Mr van Hoogstraten was a millionaire by the time he was 23 who owned 350 properties in Sussex alone. These days he is building a sprawling £30 million palace on his High Cross estate. It will be Britain's biggest private house.

And when he decided he wanted privacy, the most prized luxury this decade, a lowly public footpath was not going to get in his way. Explaining why he had surrounded the right of way with barbed wire, he declared: "The only purpose in creating wealth like mine is to separate oneself from the riff-raff." How wrong he was.

Angered by the capitalist taunts, Mr Bennett and the Ramblers Association were immediately on the war path. They made High Cross a target in their campaign to open up all rights of way by the year 2000.

The Reddish MP's track record makes him just the man for the job. Mr Bennett is a long time philanthropist who stands up for the ordinary man and woman.

Chairman of the Government's Environmental Select Committee, he has regularly spoken out on the issue of footpaths.

He has slammed cuts in lone parent benefits and called for cuts in VAT on fuel to help those on low incomes. In parliament, he has opposed fox hunting and attacked the unfair treatment building societies showed to those who bought council houses.

Speaking after the demonstration, he told the Stockport Express: "The footpath was padlocked and barbed wire covered the blocks. Gaining access was extremely difficult but we pressed on.

"Mr van Hoogstraten's behaviour is outrageous and he had to be challenged. Many local people are too afraid to use this right of way, and that is completely unacceptable.

"The network of public footpaths belongs to everyone and is part of our history. Walking the country is something everyone is entitled to, not just ramblers, and we will protect this right."

Is it worth what is going to be a lengthy and expensive battle? It is only one bit of footpath in the country. And after all, nobody wants jolly ramblers traipsing past their kitchen window, just because it happens to be a right of way.

But the right to roam is quintessentially English. And will be something of the past if van Hoogstraten is allowed to win.

The situation lies in the hands of East Sussex County Council. The next stage is for them to prosecute van Hoogstraten and legally force him to give the public right of way.

But as much as the council sympathises, funds will inevitably be stretched to the limit and the path won't be top priority. Andrew Bennett, MP can only hope the matter is taken up in parliament as a private members bill.

One thing is for sure, he won't give up.

'Rumble in the Countryside' from **The Stockport Express**

Analysing how language is used to reinforce bias

Writers often use words which emphasise their point of view.

In the article entitled 'Rumble in the Countryside', Andrew Bennett is described as a 'noble protector of Britain's humble public footpaths'. The words 'noble' and 'protector' imply that what he is doing is good and it is honourable for him to spend his time on such a worthwhile cause. The word 'humble' suggests that he is not doing it for fame and glory. The footpath he is protecting is described as 'ancient' and 'part of our history'. What do these words suggest?

Nicholas van Hoogstraten is described as the 'property tycoon and former slum landlord'. 'Property tycoon' and 'slum landlord' are placed next to each other to emphasise that, although he is very wealthy, the properties he rents are not well cared for. The use of the word 'slum' implies something unpleasant and sleazy about him. What do these words suggest about the way he treats his tenants?

In both cases the writer is using words which project a particular impression.

Activity 7

1 Find and copy two other examples of words being used to give a biased view of:
   a Andrew Bennett   **b** Nicholas van Hoogstraten.

   Highlight the important words in your examples and explain the effect they have.

2 We are told that the two men are preparing 'to do battle' and are 'irreconcilable forces'.
   a List as many other examples as you can find of this language of conflict.
   b Why do you think the writer has chosen to write in this way?
   c What effect does it have?

3 What different groups in society are Andrew Bennett and Nicholas van Hoogstraten shown to represent?

4 It is often easier for a writer to take the part of the poor man against the wealthy one. Can you make any suggestions as to why this is so?

This article claims to look at life 'from both sides of the fence'. Yet, as you have seen, it is full of bias. It is important to be able to detect bias when you are reading. You need to see the issues that lie behind the bias in order to gain a balanced point of view.

Activity 8

1 Talk about the issues being raised in this article. You should think about issues to do with:

   ◆ public footpaths   ◆ individual freedom   ◆ social class or status   ◆ race.

   For each of the four points above, jot down in note form what the writer appears to be saying about them in the article. Highlight the parts that demonstrate bias. If you have a photocopy of the article, you could highlight the different areas in different colours.

2 Discuss why the writer might have chosen to present these issues in this way.

Analysing the writer's style in more detail

The writer's style is very important. A close analysis of three paragraphs taken from 'Rumble in the Countryside' reveals certain stylistic features.

Opening of both paragraphs linked by image of a boxing match.

Adjectival phrase presented as sentence for emphasis and effect.

Mention of Nazi-speak to link van Hoogstraten with Hitler.

Adjectives used to suggest reliability.

> In the red corner stands Andrew Bennett, Labour MP for Reddish, and President of the Ramblers Association. In the true blue corner is Nicholas van Hoogstraten. [Multi-millionaire property owner.] The man who refers to ramblers in [frightening Nazi-speak] as 'the great unwashed'. He is not a man to [forgive those who trespass against him.]
>
>   The battle commenced last week when [Andrew Bennett], a lifelong and committed rambler, led a demonstration at [van Hoogstraten's] High Cross estate in East Sussex.

Sentence without a main clause, for emphasis and effect.

Religious reference to The Lord's Prayer.

Full name used to create familiarity.

Surname only used to create distance.

Activity 9 ICT

Read these different fact files.

Name	Andrew Bennett
Age	59
Status	MP and one-time teacher
Family	lives alone
Income	above average
Manner	aggressive, confrontational
Hobbies	walking across other people's homes

NAME:	Nick van Hoogstraten
AGE:	53
STATUS:	property developer
FAMILY:	wife and three children, Josh (17), Katy (11) and Kirsty (3)
INCOME:	high
MANNER:	values privacy
HOBBIES:	home and family

Write a new article, based on the same points of conflict as the article on page 117, but this time show bias in favour of Nick van Hoogstraten. Your article should be no more than 300 words.

Use the photographs above and the reworked fact files as a starting point. Aim to include some of the stylistic features used by Joanne Murphy, who wrote the original article. The main purpose of your article is to show that you understand how bias works.

The following extract is taken from Maya Angelou's autobiography, *I Know Why The Caged Bird Sings*. In this book she describes growing up in the 1930s in Arkansas, a southern state of the United States of America. This passage is set in her grandmother's store.

Looking at detail

 1 Copy the following chart. As you read the passage below, record what you find out about the store both in the mornings and in the late afternoons. Collect details on:

- what the store is like – its appearance and atmosphere
- the people, their mood, and the things they do and say.

The store in the mornings	The store in the late afternoons
Lamplight – 'soft make-believe feeling'	Dying sunlight

8 marks

p.201

I Know Why The Caged Bird Sings

Each year I watched the field across from the Store turn caterpillar green, then gradually frosty white. I knew exactly how long it would be before the big wagons would pull into the front yard and load on the cotton pickers at daybreak to carry them to the remains of **slavery's plantations**.

5 During the picking season my grandmother would get out of bed at four o'clock (she never used an alarm clock) and creak down to her knees and chant in a sleep-filled voice, 'Our Father, thank you for letting me see this New Day. Thank you that you didn't allow the bed I lay on last night to be my cooling board, nor my blanket my winding sheet. Guide my feet this day along the straight and narrow and help me to

10 put a bridle on my tongue. Bless this house, and everybody in it. Thank you, in the name of your Son, Jesus Christ, Amen.'

Before she had quite arisen, she called our names and issued orders, and pushed her large feet into homemade slippers and across the bare lye-washed wooden floor to light the coal-oil lamp.

15 The lamplight in the Store gave a soft make-believe feeling to our world which made me want to whisper and walk about on tiptoe. The odors of onions and oranges and kerosene had been mixing all night and wouldn't be disturbed until the wooded slat was removed from the door and the early morning air forced its way in with the bodies of people who had walked miles to reach the pickup place.

20 'Sister, I'll have two cans of sardines.'
'I'm gonna work so fast today I'm gonna make you look like you standing still.'
'Lemme have a hunk of cheese and some sody crackers.'

'Just gimme a coupla them fat peanut paddies.' That would be from a picker who was taking his lunch. The greasy brown paper sack was stuck behind the bib of his
25 overalls. He'd use the candy as a snack before the noon sun called the workers to rest.

In those tender mornings the Store was full of laughing, joking, boasting and bragging. One man was going to pick two hundred pounds of cotton, and another three hundred. Even the children were promising to bring home **fo' bits and six bits**.

The champion picker of the day before was the hero of the dawn. If he prophesied
30 that the cotton in today's field was going to be sparse and stick to the bolls like glue, every listener would grunt a hearty agreement.

The sound of the empty cotton sacks dragging over the floor and the murmurs of waking people were sliced by the cash register as we rang up the five-cent sales.

If the morning sounds and smells were touched with the supernatural, the late
35 afternoon had all the features of the normal Arkansas life. In the dying sunlight the people dragged, rather than their empty cotton sacks.

Brought back to the Store, the pickers would step out of the backs of trucks and fold down, dirt-disappointed, to the ground. No matter how much they had picked, it wasn't enough. Their wages wouldn't even get them out of debt to my grandmother, not to
40 mention the staggering bill that waited on them at the **white commissary** downtown.

The sounds of the new morning had been replaced with grumbles about cheating houses, weighted scales, snakes, skimpy cotton and dusty rows. In later years I was to confront the stereotyped picture of gay song-singing cotton pickers with such inordinate rage that I was told even by fellow Blacks that my paranoia was embarrassing. But I
45 had seen the fingers cut by the mean little cotton bolls, and I had witnessed the backs and shoulders and arms and legs resisting any further demands.

*from **I Know Why The Caged Bird Sings** by Maya Angelou*

Word bank
slavery's plantations – the huge farms on which cotton is grown and which, not long before, had been run on slave labour
fo' bits and six bits – small amounts of money
white commissary – a shop supplying food and/or equipment

2 Use the notes you have taken to help you write a paragraph in which you compare the store in the morning with the store in the late afternoon. Remember to:
   ◆ point out the similarities and differences
   ◆ refer to the text and use quotations effectively.

You could start your paragraph like this:

> The same people come into the store in the afternoon as in the morning but their mood is different …

The following words and phrases may help you to make comparisons:
   ◆ alternatively …   ◆ on the other hand …   ◆ similarly …
   ◆ however …   ◆ in contrast …   ◆ whereas …   **8 marks**

3 In lines 20–23 ('Sister' … 'them fat peanut paddies') Maya Angelou shows us how the cotton pickers spoke. Identify three ways in which their speech is different from standard English and explain how it is different.   **6 marks**

4 Think about the underlined phrases in the sentences below and how they are used to describe the workers. Make notes on what the words suggest to you before answering the question.

> *In the dying sunlight the people dragged, rather than their empty cotton sacks.*
>   *Brought back to the Store, the pickers would step out of the backs of trucks and fold down, dirt-disappointed, to the ground.* (lines 35–38)

What is unusual about the way the writer describes the people and their movements in each of these three phrases? What picture does she create of the workers?   **9 marks**

5 In line 16, Maya Angelou refers to the 'odors' of onions and oranges. What is different about the spelling of this word? What is the reason for this difference?   **2 marks**

6 What do you learn about the writer's culture from this passage? It will help you to think about the:
   ◆ grandmother's prayer
   ◆ different types of food
   ◆ things you learn about the way the cotton pickers live.   **8 marks**

7 In this passage, Maya Angelou describes a scene from her childhood. However, in the last paragraph her adult voice comes across very strongly.
   a What is the 'stereotyped picture' she objects to?   **2 marks**
   b What does this paragraph show you about:
   ◆ how the author feels about this stereotyped picture?
   ◆ the reasons for her feelings?
   ◆ what she is like as an adult?   **7 marks**

TOTAL 50 marks

Section D ◆ Writing non-fiction
Introduction

Throughout Key Stages 2 and 3 you will have learned that different types of non-fiction texts have their own styles and conventions, or accepted ways of writing. You will have learned how to adapt the style and structure of non-fiction texts to suit the needs of your audience and your reasons for writing. The units in this section will extend your skills in writing for a range of purposes.

In Unit 13, *Writing to inform, describe and explain*, you will learn how to organise your information clearly and adapt your style of writing according to the needs of your readers. You will learn how to use details to make information clearer for your readers. You will also learn how to structure your ideas to explain events and ideas clearly for your readers.

In Unit 14, *Presenting a persuasive speech*, you will learn how to present a case persuasively and how to use techniques that will capture the attention of your readers.

In Unit 15, *Writing to advise*, you will learn how to offer advice in both personal and impersonal ways, how to meet objections your readers might make and how to present your advice effectively.

In Unit 16, *Writing to analyse*, you will learn how to analyse situations and texts in a logical way and present your ideas and conclusions clearly based on the available evidence.

Unit 17 tests you on the skills you will develop as you work carefully through the four units.

This unit will help you to:
- ◆ organise and present information clearly
- ◆ use descriptive detail to make accounts vivid for your readers
- ◆ combine and organise information from a range of sources
- ◆ give clear and well-organised explanations.

Organising and presenting information

Unlike narrative writing, information texts are not presented in chronological order. They are not written as a clear sequence of events. The writer of an information text can decide on the order in which he or she wants to present information.

Read the text below, which has been written for a travel guide to New York. The text has been written to provide interesting information for tourists about a well-known landmark.

The Statue of Liberty

The Statue of Liberty was presented to America by the people of France in celebration of the alliance of the two nations which contributed to the United States gaining independence. In his official acceptance statement in 1886, President Cleveland said,
5 'We will not forget that liberty here made her home; nor shall her chosen altar be neglected.'

Sculptor, Frédéric Bartholdi modelled the statue, officially 'Liberty Enlightening the World', on a huge scale. Liberty is 152 feet tall, she weighs 2,225 tons, has a thirty foot waistline, her
10 index finger is eight feet long and even one of her fingernails is 13 inches long; the spikes in her crown represent either the seven oceans or continents of the world and her torch represents enlightenment. The tablet in her hand is inscribed with 'July 4, 1776', the Day of America's Independence.

Activity 1

The passage on the Statue of Liberty contains the following types of information. Put these in the order they are organised in the text. Write a number for each type to show the correct order.

physical appearance	facts and figures
when officially accepted	political importance

The aim of a tourist guide is to present useful and interesting information. Entries in tourist guides are often short so that tourists can refer to them quickly and easily. For this reason they are usually written in a very clear and simple style.

Activity 2 ICT

1 Look at the following features and decide which of them the writer has used to present information on the Statue of Liberty simply and clearly. Find an example from the text to support your decisions.

- ◆ Complex sentences using connectives such as 'although' and 'because'.
- ◆ Simple sentences containing one clause and one verb.
- ◆ Use of modal verbs such as 'may' and 'might' (to suggest possibility).
- ◆ Written in the first person, expresses feelings and opinions.
- ◆ Written in the third person.
- ◆ Informal tone using everyday vocabulary and expressions.
- ◆ Formal vocabulary to create an impersonal tone.
- ◆ Compound sentences made up of simple sentences linked by a comma, a semicolon or the simple connective 'and'.

2 What reasons might the writer have had for choosing to use some of these features in writing and not others? Think about:

- ◆ why the text has been written
- ◆ who is going to read it.

Activity 3 (WS) (ICT)

Use the picture on this page, the information on page 124 and the fact box below to write a section about the Statue of Liberty for a travel guide.

Facts

◆ Viewing galleries in torch and crown

◆ Elevator and spiral staircase

◆ Height of statue: 152 feet

◆ Museum in base

◆ Exhibitions on construction of statue, experiences of immigrants

It may help you to organise your answer in the following way.

Step 1: Make a list of features that a visitor might find interesting – for example, the spiral staircase.

Step 2: Number the features in the order you will write about them. Think about what tourists might want to do most and what they would find interesting.

Step 3: Write your information page. Remember to do the following:
◆ Begin with a general statement before you move on to specific details.
◆ Write in the present tense to describe the statue as it is now.
◆ Use the past tense if you refer to the history of the statue.
◆ Write in the third person.
◆ Vary your sentence types – for example, you can use:
  – short, simple sentences for impact or to give a direct fact: 'Her index finger is eight feet long.'
  – compound sentences to link two or more ideas: 'The statue's torch symbolizes the enlightenment; her seven-pointed crown represents the continents.'
  – complex sentences to give more information: 'The Statue of Liberty, which was officially accepted in 1886, was a gift to America from the people of France'.

Step 4: Edit and refine your work. Then review it with a partner. Compare the similarities and differences in what you have each written. Check each other's work using these questions to help you.

Does the account contain a range of details?

Does the text sound like a continuation of the one on page 124?

Is it easy for a reader to follow and understand the information?

Is the spelling and punctuation accurate?

Step 5: Take into account any suggestions from your partner, then write the final version of your piece.

Using descriptive details to make accounts vivid

Read the extract below in which a writer recounts her first trip to the United States and the Statue of Liberty. The passage is taken from a book of travel writing that has been written to entertain as well as inform.

This text is different from the formal information text you have just been working on, although the topic, the Statue of Liberty, is the same. It is different from the previous text because the writer includes her personal opinions and feelings about the place she has visited. She includes descriptive details to help her readers picture the scene very clearly. These do not just focus on facts, but give her personal view of what she has seen.

Activity 4 ⓦⓢ

Copy the chart below, then use it to help you understand the features of texts written to inform and entertain. Some examples have been included. Add more of your own.

Feature	Example
First person pronoun	
Use of past tense	
Descriptive details to make account personal	the sun sparkled … (line 3)
Adjectives used emotively to reveal writer's feelings	awesome (line 6)

Impressions of America

I shall never forget my first sight of the Statue of Liberty. **As we approached the statue by boat**, the sun sparkled off the headdress making it look like a giant star. I had never
5 seen a larger statue. It towered above us as we got out of the boat. It was awesome.

I spent a whole morning in the fascinating museum at the base of the statue learning about the **harrowing** experiences of the
10 immigrants who started a new life in America.

Afterwards we climbed the steep spiral stairs to the viewing gallery in the statue's torch. Although I have always been afraid of heights, I was entranced by the spectacular
15 view over the river and towards the New York skyline.

Word bank
harrowing – painful, difficult

Activity 5

With a partner make a list of the differences in the passage on page 128 and the tourist guide on page 124. Think about:

◆ the purpose of each text – why it was written
◆ the tone of each text – whether it is personal or impersonal
◆ which text uses more facts than opinions and which one more opinions than facts
◆ which text uses adjectives to make the descriptions more detailed.

Looking closely at sentences

Complex sentences consist of a main clause and one or more subordinate clauses that are linked by a connective. Using complex sentences enables writers to combine several ideas in one sentence.

Activity 6

Look again at 'Impressions of America' (page 128), where the first complex sentence in the text has been underlined. The subordinate clause has been highlighted in bold type.

1 Find and write down two complex sentences from paragraphs 1 and 3. Underline the subordinate clause in each sentence.

2 You will notice that in some sentences the subordinate clause can come in a different position in the sentence.
   a Rewrite the sentences you identified in question 1 putting the subordinate clause in a different position.
   b Discuss with a partner what difference this has made to the sentences.

3 Read the passage below, which is the first draft of an account written by a student about a recent trip to the Eiffel Tower. You will notice that only simple sentences are used in this account. Rewrite the account using some compound and complex sentences that combine ideas and connect the detail in the account.

A trip to remember

I climbed the Eiffel Tower on a Friday morning. It was quite cold. I was a bit nervous. I really wanted to climb the tower. The lift was old and rusty. It was a bit like a cage. You could see out of the sides. I didn't want to look around me. My friends wanted to travel the last bit to the top by stairs.

I began to feel more and more nervous. At the top I dared to look around. You could see for miles. You could see the river Seine with little boats on it. You could also see all the cars. They looked like little toys.

I was pleased that I had done it.

Adding descriptive detail

Descriptive details help your readers to imagine the scene you are describing more easily. They are details that focus very clearly on a particular aspect of a description. For example, the writer of 'Impressions of America' (page 128) referred to the sun sparkling on the water.

Activity 7

Look again at your version of the Eiffel Tower passage. Add some descriptive details using the list below to help you. You may add as many words as you like and miss out parts of the text if you wish.

	details about the weather
	details about your feelings
	journey to top/lift or stairs
	details about the view
	your feelings at the end of the trip

It may help you to organise your answer in the following way:

Step 1: Begin with an opening statement which sets a personal tone – for example, *I shall never forget …*

↓

Step 2: Include a range of descriptive details such as whether the wind was blowing, the view from the top and so on.

↓

Step 3: Use vocabulary emotively to make feelings clear to readers – for example, the word 'frightening'.

↓

Step 4: Include more personal opinions.

↓

Step 5: When you have finished, show your work to a partner. Ask him or her to help you check whether you have included enough details to make the account lively and interesting. Could you have used more effective vocabulary? Use a thesaurus to help you.

↓

Step 6: When you have made your alterations, write the final draft.

Combining and organising information from a range of sources

Encyclopaedias are written to inform readers about a wide range of subjects. Your next task is to research information for an encyclopaedia entry on the *Mary Celeste*, a nineteenth-century cargo ship whose crew and passengers disappeared mysteriously. With this information you will write your account, which should include details on the background to the ship, the voyage itself and how it ended.

Activity 8

1 Select the information from Sources 1 to 8 that will be most useful for your task and make notes on it.

2 You have been asked to write a *factual* account. As you read, use the headings below to help you make notes quickly and clearly. Remember that an encyclopaedia entry contains more facts than opinions. When you study the information you should try to distinguish what is fact and what is opinion in each of the sources. Remember also that notes are brief. You do not need to write full sentences.

Who?   What?   When?   Why?   Where?   How?

Source 1: Fact file source

Name of ship: *Mary Celeste*
Date of departure: 7 November 1872
Port of departure: New York
Destination: Genoa, Italy
Cargo: 1,700 barrels of raw American alcohol
Captain of ship: Captain Benjamin Briggs (aged 37); had previously captained three other ships
First mate: Albert Richardson
Second mate: A. Gilling
Cook: E. W. Head
Other crew members: V. Lorenzen and B. Lorenzen (brothers), A. Marten, G. Goodschall
Passengers: Mrs Briggs and Sophie, wife and two-year-old daughter of Captain Briggs
Discovery: 5 December 1872 by Captain Morehouse, the captain of another ship, the *Dei Gratia*, following a similar route to the *Mary Celeste*.

Notes
◆ Sailors from the *Dei Gratia* found no sign of crew of the *Mary Celeste*.
◆ The boat appeared to be seaworthy.
◆ No trace of the crew was ever found.

Tressell Publications 1981 (text produced for school students)

Source 2: Letters from Captain Briggs to his mother

It has been very **confining** for Sophie but I hope when we return we can make up for it. We seem to have a very good mate and Steward and I hope we shall have a pleasant voyage.

Word bank
confining – restricting

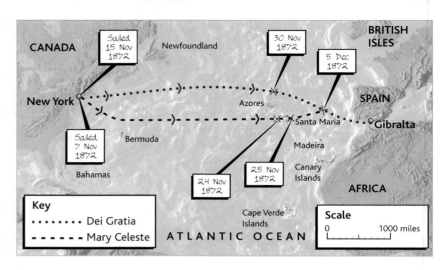

Source 3: Letter from T. Nickelson to the American Consul in Gibraltar

The mother of the two brethren (Volkert and Bob Lorenzen) is still living and she does not cease to **deplore** the loss of her two sons. That some must have lost their lives, I take as a fact, but I cannot admit that they have had a share in any act of violence or in any **mutiny** which is guaranteed to me the character of the men in question who were of a most **pacific** disposition.

Word bank
deplore – be very upset by
mutiny – uprising by the crew of a ship
pacific – peaceful

Source 4: Comments to newspaper by Mrs Richardson, wife of the first mate

Word bank
presentiment – feeling beforehand

'I always believed and always will believe that my husband, Captain Briggs, Mrs. Briggs, her baby and the cook were murdered by the crew,' Mrs Richardson told The Eagle's reporter. Her husband, she stated, had a presentiment of evil before he sailed, and he appeared to her in a dream on the night of 24th November, the date on which she believed the catastrophe occurred.

Source 5: Statements from the Court of Enquiry

Oliver Deveau (sailor from the Dei Gratia who boarded the Mary Celeste)

The jib and the fore-topsail were set. All the other sails were furled. The rigging on the port side was broken. The starboard lower topsail brace was broken, the main peak halyard was broken and the gear of the foresail.

Word bank
furled – rolled up
rigging – ropes
port – left-hand side of the boat as seen from the stern
starboard – right-hand side of the boat
brace – rope for fastening the sail
halyard – rope for raising the sail

Source 6: Statements from the Court of Enquiry

John Wright
I could not tell whether any (life)boat had or had not been there at all. There were no davits on the quarter of the vessel. I saw nothing from which I could judge whether a boat had been upon deck. I saw no ropes on either side showing that a boat had been launched from the ship at all. I observed no remains of any tow line.

Word bank
davits – used for lowering a lifeboat

Source 7: Letter from Gibraltar's Attorney-General to the American Consul in Gibraltar

On examining the starboard topgallant sail, marks were discovered, apparently of blood, and a mark of a blow, and apparently of a sharp one. On descending through the fore-hatch, a barrel, ostensibly of alcohol, appeared to be tampered with.

Word bank
topgallant sail – the sail above the top mast sail
ostensibly – appearing to be

Source 8: Meteorological report

The records of the Servicio Meterologico in the Azores say that the weather deteriorated that morning and a storm blew up involving gale force winds and torrential rain. The Captain of the *Dei Gratia* says in his sworn record that the weather had been blowing very hard for seven or eight days previous and had only moderated in the morning of the 4th.

Activity 9

1 Now that you have completed your notes, think about each source of information and how reliable it might be. Show your notes to a partner and grade each piece of information for reliability using this code:

   a very reliable　　　**b** reasonably reliable　　　**c** not reliable at all.

2 Why is it important that an encyclopaedia should contain reliable information?

3 Revise your notes to check that you have not recorded the same information more than once.

   ◆ Have you recorded any information that is not relevant?
   ◆ Are there any gaps in your notes?
   ◆ Do you need to go back and fill in any missing information?

4 Before you write your encyclopaedia entry, look at this example which has been annotated to show you how the writing has been organised.

The Bermuda Triangle

This is a region of the western Atlantic Ocean lying roughly between 30 degrees and 40 degrees latitude in which numerous ships have vanished without trace. The Bermuda Triangle is also known as the Devils' Triangle and covers about 1,140,000 sq km between the island of Bermuda, the coast of Florida and Puerto Rico.

The sinister reputation of the Bermuda Triangle may be traceable to reports made in the late fifteenth century by navigator Christopher Colombus in which floating masses of gulfweed were regarded as uncanny and perilous by early sailors. Others date the notoriety of the area to the mid nineteenth century when a number of reports were made of unexplained disappearances and mysteriously abandoned ships.

Annotations (left):
- Use of present tense to describe how things are.
- Uses complex sentence to add extra information.
- Uses dates to guide reader through sequence of events.
- Uses past tense to describe events that have already happened.
- Conclusion summarises what people believed about the Bermuda Triangle.

Annotations (right):
- Gives specific details of place
- Uses modal ver to suggest possibility/to s this is not a fac

Using non-factual information in an encyclopaedia entry

You will have noticed from the annotations in Activity 9 that the modal verb 'may' has been used to show that a piece of information that may not be a fact has been used in the entry on the Bermuda Triangle.

Activity 10

You need to be able to write your encyclopaedia entry without misleading your readers. Select two pieces of information on your 'not reliable' list (see Activity 9), then write a sentence for each one using one of these modal verbs:

◆ may   ◆ might   ◆ could.

Activity 11 (WS)

Now that you have refined your information about the *Mary Celeste*, use the Bermuda Triangle extract as a model to write your own encyclopaedia entry.

Inform your readers about the ship itself, its voyage, the passengers and crew, and its eventual fate. Build in the two sentences you have just practised, which use modal verbs. It may help you to organise your piece in the following way:

Step 1: Use your notes to plan your writing. Think about the order in which you want to present the information to your readers. Remember that information texts do not always follow a chronological order (one that arranges events in the order they happened).

Make sure you have included all the relevant information about the *Mary Celeste*. Also make sure that you have not included the same information more than once.

Step 2: Refer to this checklist as you write:

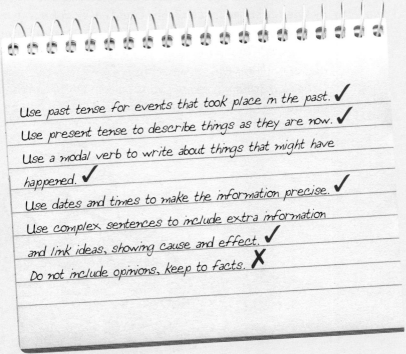

Use past tense for events that took place in the past. ✔
Use present tense to describe things as they are now. ✔
Use a modal verb to write about things that might have happened. ✔
Use dates and times to make the information precise. ✔
Use complex sentences to include extra information and link ideas, showing cause and effect. ✔
Do not include opinions, keep to facts. ✗

Step 3: When you have written your first draft, give your work to a partner to read. Ask your partner to check that:

◆ s/he can understand your information easily

◆ your information is so clearly presented s/he could use it to inform someone else about the *Mary Celeste*

◆ your account tells your readers everything they need to know about the ship and its voyage.

Step 4: Make any alterations necessary. Then write the final draft.

Writing to explain

An explanation tells readers how and why things happen or how something works. It makes links for readers between causes and their effects. Words that link the cause and effect are known as 'causal connectives'.

Activity 12

1 In the following explanation, the causal connectives have been missed out. As you read, match the numbers in the text with the correct causal connective from the list below.

> Many theories exist to explain the disappearance of ships in the Bermuda Triangle. It is possible that tropical storms are responsible for the destruction of ships in the area. Tropical storms can build up very quickly and **1** they are not always detected by satellite surveillance. **2** they *could* easily sink a ship without trace.
>
> Scientists have found that there is a great deal of seismic activity in the area. <u>It is possible</u> that **3** this activity, underwater earthquakes are causing ships and planes to disappear.
>
> The Gulf Stream is a very strong current which can throw sailors off course **4** they do not know how to compensate for it. **5** ships <u>might</u> be destroyed in the area of the Bermuda Triangle.

Causal connectives:

◆ as a result of   ◆ so   ◆ in this way   ◆ therefore   ◆ because

2 Three parts of the text have been underlined. Can you explain why they are all similar? Why are these words and phrases useful when you are writing explanations?

Activity 13

Work with a partner to prepare an explanation for what happened to those on board the *Mary Celeste*. Your explanation will take the form of a formal spoken presentation to your class with the title:

> *What happened to the* Mary Celeste*? Our theory*

It may help you to organise your presentation in the following way:

Step 1: Look back at the notes you made earlier on the *Mary Celeste* and also at the source material (pages 131–133).

◆ You will notice that some pieces of evidence are in conflict (disagree) with others.
◆ Discuss with your partner which of these particular pieces of evidence are most likely to be reliable and why.

Step 2: Make a plan following these guidelines:

Opening paragraph Introduce the mystery of the *Mary Celeste* to your audience. You may use some of the illustrations in this section as visual aids to your presentation.

Paragraph 2 Refer to the evidence that you consider unreliable. Explain to your listeners what might have happened to the crew and passengers if this evidence is to be believed. For example, the fact that the alcohol barrels had been tampered with could be used to explain that some of the crew got drunk and had a fight, which resulted in them falling overboard.

Paragraph 3 Refer to the evidence you both consider to be reliable. Use this evidence to explain to your audience what could have happened to the *Mary Celeste*.

Conclusion Sum up your evidence giving a final explanation for your theory of what happened to the *Mary Celeste*.

Step 3: Make your presentation. Remember to:

◆ use causal connectives such as 'because', 'so', 'as a result of' and 'to'
◆ use modal verbs such as 'could', 'may', and 'might' to suggest possibility
◆ use sentence starters such as 'It is possible that ...' and 'Maybe ...'
◆ avoid using the vocabulary and sentence structures of everyday conversation – remember, this is a formal presentation.

Divide the presentation between the two of you. One way to do this is for one person to deal with the unreliable evidence and for the other to deal with the reliable evidence on which your final explanation will depend.

Remember to speak confidently and to make eye contact with your audience as you give your explanation.

This unit will help you to:
- ◆ organise and structure your ideas when writing a speech
- ◆ understand how to use rhetorical devices
- ◆ use the passive voice for effect
- ◆ present a case persuasively.

Planning to make an impact

When you make a speech it is very important to plan and structure your ideas so that you can make an impact on your audience. Before you make a formal speech to your audience, you need to produce a written version so you can structure your ideas carefully and revise them.

Read this extract from *Animal Farm* by George Orwell. *Animal Farm* is a famous novel written in 1945, in which farm animals rebel against the human beings who control them. In the novel, Old Major, the pig, makes a powerful speech persuading the animals to rebel against their owner, the cruel farmer Mr Jones.

Read the speech with a partner and answer the questions as you read to help you understand how it is structured.

The struggle

Now comrades, what is the nature of this life of ours? Let us face it, our lives are miserable, **laborious** and short.

We are born, we are given just so much food as will keep the breath in our bodies, and those of us who are capable of it are
5 forced to work to the last **atom** of our strength; and the very instant that our usefulness has come to an end we are slaughtered with hideous cruelty. No animal in England knows the meaning of happiness or leisure after he is a year old. No animal in England is free. The life of an animal is misery and
10 slavery: that is the plain truth.

What is the idea that Old Major wants his audience to consider in the opening to the speech? Why is it important to begin a speech with a powerful idea?

The main idea from the opening paragraph is developed in this section. Write down three examples of this development. How does the writer repeat the first idea at the end of this paragraph?

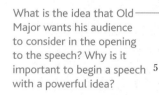

When you make a speech you want your audience to think or behave differently as a result of hearing your speech. How does Old Major try to influence the behaviour of his audience here?

How does the writer draw his ideas together in the final paragraph? What does he want his audience to think or do at the end of his speech?

… And remember, comrades, your resolution must never falter. No argument must lead you astray. Never listen when they tell you that Man and the animals have a common interest, that the prosperity of the one is the prosperity of the others. It is all lies.

15   Man serves the interests of no creature except himself. And among us animals let there be perfect unity, perfect comradeship to the struggle. All men are enemies. All animals are comrades.

*from **Animal Farm** by George Orwell*

Word bank
laborious – involving hard work
atom – smallest particle

Activity 1 ICT

Using the same structure as in the speech from *Animal Farm*, plan the outline of a speech of your own. Your task is to persuade your fellow students to campaign with you for an extra two weeks' school holiday at the end of the school year. Use the headings below.

Opening paragraph, my main idea

Three examples to develop my main idea

Ideas for getting my audience on my side

My final message

Getting the attention of your audience

Rhetorical devices are particular ways of using words to get the attention of your audience. They are very effective ways of persuading your audience to pay attention to your speech.

Look at Old Major's speech in more detail to understand how the writer has used rhetorical devices.

Activity 2 (WS) (ICT)

Make a chart like the one below. Then work with a partner and re-read the speech from *Animal Farm* on pages 138–139 to find an example to match each of the rhetorical devices listed. Explain their effect on the audience. The first one has been done for you.

Device	Example	Effect on the audience
Appealing directly to reader	'Now comrades' (line 1)	Makes them feel they are his friends
Asking a rhetorical question		
Using pronouns 'we' and 'us'		
Using language emotively to appeal to your readers' feelings		

Activity 3 (WS)

1 Write your own introduction to the speech you planned in Activity 1. Use the rhetorical devices from the chart you made in Activity 2 to help you get your audience on your side. Aim to write no more than two or three sentences. Use the guidelines below.

Guidelines

◆ Before you begin, think about your **purpose**, which is to **persuade** all students of your age to share your opinions and campaign for longer holidays.

◆ Think also about your **audience: students of your own age**.

◆ Appeal directly to your audience using phrases such as 'friends' or 'fellow school students'.

◆ Aim to use one of the following words at least once: 'we', 'us', 'ours'.

◆ Use a rhetorical question such as: 'We all suffer from overwork, don't we?'

◆ Use language emotively to appeal to the feelings of your audience.

◆ Try to use words in groups of three: think of a suitable starter word like 'tired', then use a thesaurus to find other adjectives for your group of three.

2 When you have finished, pass your paragraph to a partner to read. Then ask your partner if s/he can spot the rhetorical devices you have used.

Extending your knowledge of rhetorical devices

Once you have grabbed the attention of your audience and set a tone for your speech, you should develop your ideas in more detail, continuing to use rhetorical devices to keep your audience's attention.

Re-read the second paragraph of Old Major's speech, shown again below. The writer builds on the devices used in the opening to explain more clearly to the animals why their lives are so miserable.

The plain truth

We are born, we are given just so much food as will keep the breath in our bodies, and those of us who are capable of it are forced to work to the last atom of our strength; and the very instant that our usefulness has come to an end we are slaughtered with hideous cruelty. No animal in England knows the
5   meaning of happiness or leisure after he is a year old. No animal in England is free. The life of an animal is misery and slavery: that is the plain truth.

*from **Animal Farm** by George Orwell*

Activity 4 Ⓘ

As you read the passage above, pick out the words or phrases which fit the descriptions in the list below.

a language used emotively   b sentence beginnings repeated for effect
c short sentence to sum up final message   d exaggeration for effect
e groups of three   f use of the passive voice, placing emphasis on the use of 'we'

Activity 5

Continue your speech to persuade your fellow students to campaign for longer holidays in the summer by developing your ideas in more detail. Aim to write two more paragraphs.

1 Write down four ideas you intend to use.

2 Number the ideas in order of importance.

3 Write ideas for short sentences to sum up your message.
   Don't forget:

   ◆ groups of three: 'All year we work, we struggle with homework and ...'
   ◆ exaggeration: 'It is time this cruelty to school students is stopped'
   ◆ repetition: 'No student can be expected to ... No student should be expected to ...'
   ◆ a short snappy sentence to sum up your ideas: 'We work hard; we deserve a rest'
   ◆ use of the passive voice to emphasise what is being done to you and to place emphasis on subject 'we': 'We are made to ...'.

Finishing your speech effectively

The ending of a speech is your last opportunity to get your audience on your side. Read the ending of Old Major's speech, shown again below.

Resolutions

And remember, comrades, your resolution must never falter. No argument must lead you astray. Never listen when they tell you that Man and the animals have a common interest, that the prosperity of the one is the prosperity of the others. It is all lies.

5   Man serves the interests of no creature except himself. And among us animals let there be perfect unity, perfect comradeship to the struggle. All men are enemies. All animals are comrades.

*from **Animal Farm** by George Orwell*

Activity 6 (WS)

As you read this final part of Old Major's speech, see if you can find examples of:

◆ two imperatives (verbs that tell the audience directly what to do)
◆ short sentences to sum up key ideas
◆ use of contrasting vocabulary that shows the difference between the humans and the animals
◆ use of commas that help readers to pause at important points.

Activity 7

Now write the final paragraph of your speech getting your fellow students to campaign for an extra two weeks' summer holiday. Use the guidelines to help you.

Guidelines

◆ Be direct with your audience. Give them orders using the imperative form of the verb – for example: 'Join with me in ...', and 'Do not listen to those who say ...'.
◆ Aim to use contrasting ideas.
◆ Finish with a clear reminder of the issue you are campaigning for: 'Students everywhere must unite to demand longer holidays.'

Redrafting and refining your work

Show the whole of your speech to a partner and ask him or her to mark on the text where you have used:

◆ different rhetorical devices
◆ vocabulary to appeal to your readers' emotions
◆ varied sentence structures including questions and short sentences
◆ commas to make your readers pause at important points.

Discuss with your partner any alterations you may need to make. Then read your speech aloud to your partner. Does it sound persuasive enough? If the answer is 'Yes', write the final draft.

15 Writing to advise

This unit will help you to:

◆ adapt your writing to different audiences

◆ make use of different presentational devices

◆ use an impersonal tone when offering advice

◆ use argument and counter-argument to meet the objections of your readers.

Adapting your writing to your audience

The way in which you give advice depends on the audience you are writing for and your purpose.

The advice below to parents is taken from a leaflet about drugs and solvents. The tone is serious and formal. The text has been annotated to show you how it has been structured and how the formal tone is achieved.

Activity 1

As you read the text below, answer the questions that are shown around it.

Begins by showing understanding of readers' difficulties. Can you find another place in the text where the writer does this?

Formal vocabulary suited to adult audience. Can you find other examples in this text?

Advice begins here.

The advice is set out differently in this section. Can you work out why?

LIFE CAN BE DIFFICULT FOR PARENTS

It's not easy to be always available for your children. So it's important to talk and listen to them when you are available. If they feel you are interested in their views and in their problems, they'll be much more likely to confide in you. You might then be able to influence whether or not they experiment with drugs, or help them if they've already started, and at least make sure they are well informed. However reluctant you may be, it's far better to talk about the problem with your child.

◆ Talk with them about their feelings on drugs.

◆ Get them to think about how they might refuse drugs.

◆ Listen and take your children seriously.

◆ Set an example. The way you use alcohol, tobacco and medicines is an example to your children.

Looking more closely at sentence structure

The text on page 143 uses a variety of sentence structures to get advice across to readers.

◆ **'Life can be difficult for parents'** is a simple sentence that consists of one clause. This is an effective way to begin this particular text because it provides a clear and simple introduction to the topic, the difficulty that some parents have in talking to their children about drugs.

◆ **'So it's important to talk and listen to them when you are available'** is a complex sentence consisting of a main clause 'So it's important' and a subordinate clause 'when you are available'. The main clause could make a sentence on its own. The subordinate clause would not make a sentence on its own, but gives additional information about the main clause. In this case, the subordinate clause is used to show that the writer understands there may be demands on parents' time.

◆ **'If they feel you are interested in their views and in their problems, they'll be much more likely to confide in you'** is also a complex sentence. The subordinate clause beginning with 'if' is a subtle and indirect way of giving advice. This sentence shows how if one course of action is taken, then another is likely to follow. Parents are being advised to take an interest in what their children say and as a result their children will be more likely to confide in them.

◆ **'Talk with them about their feelings'** appears in the second section of the text. In this section, the advice is given much more directly. This sentence and the others in this section are imperatives: they give instructions.

Activity 2

1 Write your own simple sentence addressed to parents. Your sentence will form the first part of an advice leaflet called 'Drugs: A Parents' Guide.'

2 Complete the gaps in this complex sentence with ideas of your own. This sentence will be part of your advice leaflet.

> It is important to .... when ....

3 Write your own sentence addressed to parents for your advice leaflet using this model:

> If .... then they will ....

4 Write your own sentence using an imperative to give advice to parents when talking to their children about drugs.

Activity 3

Now use the information in this box to write a whole paragraph for your advice leaflet, 'Drugs: A Parents' Guide'. The heading for this section is 'How Do You Know If Your Child Is Using Drugs?'

Facts

◆ Mood changes – from happy to sad

◆ Loss of appetite

◆ No interest in hobbies, schoolwork, sport or friends

◆ Falling asleep

◆ Unexplained loss of money or belongings from the home

Use the following sentence as your starter sentence:

Young people sometimes experiment with drugs.

It may help to organise your writing in the following way:

Step 1: Remember to:

◆ keep your audience in mind (parents)

◆ show that you understand the difficulties your readers might have

◆ use formal vocabulary – avoid using slang

◆ state facts rather than opinions: instead of 'I think ...', use a phrase such as 'It can be seen that ...'

◆ write mostly in the present tense

◆ appeal to your readers directly using the words 'you' or 'your children'

◆ use a variety of sentences; build in the ones you have just practised.

Step 2: Redraft and refine your work. When you have finished, read your work aloud to a partner. Then ask him or her to find at least one example of each of the following in your work:

◆ appropriate vocabulary for an adult audience

◆ different sentence types

◆ places where you have appealed to your audience directly.

Step 3: Make any alterations you and your partner think are necessary before you produce the final draft.

Using an informal tone

The text below is taken from the introduction to an advice leaflet on drugs entitled 'The Score'. The writer of the text has used an informal tone to offer advice to a teenage audience.

A text written in an informal style sounds like ordinary speech. It sounds as if the writer is talking directly to the reader. A text with an informal tone is more likely to use:

◆ the vocabulary and expressions of everyday speech
◆ punctuation that helps the reader to pause as people do when they are talking
◆ uncomplicated sentence structures such as you would use in ordinary conversation.

Activity 4

As you read the text below, answer the questions to help you work out what makes this text informal in tone. Note down your answers under these headings:

◆ Everyday expressions.
◆ Compound sentences using simple connectives.
◆ Use of punctuation.

An everyday expression that you would hear in conversation. How many more of these can you find in this text?

Compound sentence. These can be joined by 'and', 'but', 'or' and also by commas or semicolons. Can you find another compound sentence? What is used to join its clauses?

The dash indicates a pause similar to a pause in conversation. What other punctuation mark is used to give the text a conversational feel?

DRUGS? WHAT'S THE BIG DEAL?

Everyone has something to say about drugs. Even so, it's still an issue wrapped in myths, and often fiction gets in the way of facts.

Knowing the score isn't just about knowing the buzz different drugs can give. It's also about being aware of the effects they can have on your mind, your body and even the way you live your life. There are serious risks linked to drug taking, so it's vital to get your hands on information you can trust …

'The Score' puts you squarely in the picture about drugs. It answers questions, sorts problems, explains the risks and drops in on dilemmas and debates.

Whatever your viewpoint – there's something inside for everyone.

*from **The Score: Facts About Drugs** by National Drugs Helpline*

Activity 5 (WS) (ICT)

Use the information in the box below to write the first draft of a page for a booklet advising young people not to take drugs to improve their sporting performance. Aim to write three or four short paragraphs.

Facts

◆ Taking drugs to improve performance is cheating.

◆ Taking drugs can result in more injuries to the drug-taker.

◆ Anabolic steroids are dangerous for young people's health and can stop normal growth. Boys can grow breasts and girls more body hair.

◆ Discovery of drug-taking results in the drug-taker being banned from the sport.

◆ Fitness, concentration and commitment are as important as winning.

You will notice that the text on page 146 uses short paragraphs to ensure readers can access information easily and quickly. Organise your writing in the following way:

Step 1: Remember to:

◆ use everyday expressions and language

◆ use a variety of sentence types – for example, simple sentences for emphasis and snappy effects, compound sentences for linking ideas and complex sentences for providing results or causes

◆ use punctuation such as question marks and dashes, which make the reader pause as in ordinary conversation.

Step 2: Look at the words below for inspiration.

cheating	failure	dangerous	stupid
influenced	unfair	enjoyment	damaging
success	self-respect	inadvisable	sensible

If some of these words sound too formal for your piece, think of synonyms that are more likely to be heard in everyday speech.

Step 3: When you have completed your draft, ask your partner to underline places where you have:

◆ used informal language

◆ used punctuation correctly.

Appropriate presentation and structure

The next stage in presenting a text is to look at the way it appears on the page to the reader. Writers choose the most appropriate layout for their purpose to get the attention of their readers. Choosing the right font, letter size, punctuation, spacing and colour can all influence the way readers respond to written material. These are known as **presentational devices**.

Look closely at the text below, which is the one that you worked on on page 146. Here it looks very different and is more likely to have an impact on readers because of the way it is presented.

DRUGS? WHAT'S THE
BIG DEAL...?

EVERYONE has something to say about drugs. Even so, it's still an issue wrapped in *Myths*, and often **fiction** gets in the way of the FACTS.

Knowing the SCORE isn't just about knowing the buzz different drugs can give. It's also about being aware of the effects they can have on your mind, your body and even the way you live your life. There are SERIOUS risks linked to drug taking, so it's VITAL to get your hands on information you can TRUST...

The SCORE puts you squarely in the picture about drugs. It answers QUESTIONS, sorts PROBLEMS, explains the RISKS and drops in on *dilemmas* and DEBATES. Whatever your viewpoint — there's something inside for everyone.

And if it's **pure info** you're after, our DRUG FILES are one essential source you'll return to again and again. You'll find no preaching here — the FACTS speak for themselves.

Activity 6 (WS) (ICT)

Work with a partner to make a list of the ways in which the writer has used presentational devices to appeal to his audience. Make your lists under the following headings:

Use of colour	Text layout	Use of punctuation

Activity 7

Look again at the text you wrote on drugs in sport in Activity 5. Your task is to re-present this text using the techniques you have just identified. Use the text on page 148 as a model and follow the steps below.

Step 1: You will need to think about the following.

◆ The needs of your audience. What sort of presentation will appeal to them?
◆ The background colour for your text.
◆ The headings and how you will emphasise them.
◆ The words you want to emphasise in the text and how you will do this.
◆ Use of colour and different fonts to make different words stand out.
◆ How to use punctuation such as question marks, dashes and ellipses to emphasise your meaning.
◆ How and where you will use underlining.

This will be your first draft so do not spend a lot of time perfecting your design at this stage.

Step 2: Redraft and refine your work. Begin by working on the written text. Check that:

◆ you have used a variety of sentences to put your ideas across
◆ you have used language that is used by young people
◆ your paragraphs are short
◆ your text has a conversational tone
◆ you have written mainly in the present tense (remember that you use the present to describe the way things are now – for example, drugs are dangerous).

Step 3: Show your work to a partner. Then ask him or her to spot where you have used presentational techniques to attract the attention of your audience.

Step 4: Now look closely at the presentation of your text. Check that:

◆ your text looks interesting enough to attract your readers' attention
◆ your headings stand out clearly and attract attention to the key points
◆ you have used different sizes and fonts to draw attention to key words
◆ you have used punctuation to emphasise your meaning.

Step 5: When you have made any alterations you think necessary, present the final draft.

Using argument and counter-argument

Sometimes giving advice can be difficult. Sometimes the person you are advising has an answer ready for everything you tell him or her. If you want to persuade that person to take your advice you need to have your answers ready for his or her objections. You will remember that arguing against a point somebody makes is known as using **counter-argument**.

Activity 8

Look at the following comments made by a group of young people in a discussion on alcohol. Match up the comments made by Group A (letters a to d) with the answers given by Group B (numbered 1 to 4).

Group A

a You can have a good party without alcohol.
b It's illegal to buy alcohol under the age of 18.
c Alcohol affects your judgement, making you do things you might regret later.
d Alcohol leads to trouble with the police.

Group B

1 Drinking is part of growing up. No one bothers about age limits.
2 Everyone does silly things when they are young, it doesn't matter.
3 You have more fun when you drink. There's nothing wrong with having a laugh.
4 Not everyone who drinks gets into trouble with the police.

Separating argument and counter-argument

When you make counter-arguments in writing, using a comma separates the opposing sides of the argument and emphasises them both. For example:

You say you have more fun when you have a drink, **but** you should remember that it can lead to lots of problems.

Notice that the comma separates the two sides of the argument. The word 'but' signals the start of the counter-argument.

Other words that can signal the start of a counter-argument are:

◆ although ◆ on the other hand ◆ alternatively.

Can you think of any more?

Activity 9

Look back at the arguments and answers you matched in Activity 8. Rewrite each pair of sentences as an argument and counter-argument. To do this you may have to change the words a little. For example:

It can be good fun to have a drink, **but remember** you can **still** have a good party without alcohol.

The words that have been added here have been highlighted to show you how the sentences can be changed slightly.

Activity 10

Read this letter written by a teenager. The text has been annotated to show you how the letter is structured.

Introduces problem.

Parents' objections.

Elaborates on problem.

Writer's feelings.

> Dear Paul,
> I need some advice about dealing with my parents.
> [Everyone else in my class goes to parties and drinks and has a good time.] [My parents won't let me go to parties because they say everyone will be drinking and I'm not allowed to.] [They say there's always trouble at parties where people drink and they don't want me drinking under the age of 18.]
> [I'm missing out on a lot of fun because my parents are mean and old-fashioned.]
> What can I do?
>
> A bored and lonely teenager.

Write the reply from Paul. Your task is to help the letter writer to realise that his parents could have a point and perhaps he is too young to drink. You will have to expect that your reader may not be very pleased with your advice, so you need to present your ideas in a way that he will accept. You should show that you sympathise with him and agree that he has a point before you put the other side of the argument. Follow the pattern below.

Paragraph 1   Write an opening statement to show that you understand Bored and Lonely's problem. Refer to the points made in the first two sentences of the letter.

Paragraph 2   Give your advice to Bored and Lonely using counter-argument to make him see that his parents may have a point. His parents make three objections. Answer each of these in turn.

Paragraph 3   Write a concluding statement that tries to persuade Bored and Lonely to accept your advice. Refer to the point he makes in the conclusion to his letter.

Writing tips

◆   Use a friendly tone.

◆   Write mainly in the present tense.

◆   Use connectives that signal the start of your counter-argument – for example 'but' and 'however'.

◆   Use commas to separate argument and counter-argument.

Presenting advice in an impersonal way

So far you have directed your advice at a particular audience. You have addressed your readers in a personal way by using the pronoun 'you' and by using the sort of language that particular groups of readers can relate to.

Sometimes advice can be presented in an impersonal way, by not being addressed to a particular group of readers. With this kind of advice the reader may have to 'read between the lines'. For example, the statement 'Drinking too much can lead to lack of consciousness' has the hidden advice 'don't drink too much or this could happen to you'.

Take a look at the text below, which is written in an impersonal way.

Alcohol Facts

Alcohol is a depressant drug. It slows down the nervous system, reactions and the way the body functions. Drinking too much can lead to lack of consciousness. Users then risk choking on their own vomit. This can kill.

A thousand children are admitted to hospital each year with acute alcoholic poisoning. Around half of all pedestrians aged 16 to 60 killed in road accidents have more alcohol in their blood stream than the legal drink-drive limit.

Alcohol can affect how people feel, what they do and why they do things. It's something to treat with respect and to be in control of. Making decisions and learning to be in control is part of becoming an adult. Young people and their parents are both involved in allowing this to happen.

Activity 11 (WS) (ICT)

Look back at the letter you wrote to Bored and Lonely (see pages 151–152). This letter was addressed to one particular person and had a friendly personal tone. 'Alcohol Facts' opposite is written in an impersonal style.

1 Work out how the texts differ by making a chart like the one below, then completing it.

Feature	Examples in letter	Examples in 'Alcohol Facts'
Opinions		
Facts		
Reader addressed in personal way		
Use of formal language		
Use of informal language		
Direct advice given to reader		
Indirect advice given to reader		

2 Which text is more impersonal and formal? How can you tell?

Activity 12 (WS)

Use the facts in the list below to write two paragraphs in an **impersonal** style for an advice leaflet on solvents. Your audience is anyone who needs advice on these topics, either parents or young people. It is not addressed to any particular group of readers.

Solvents fact list

- Sniffed or breathed into lungs

- Illegal for shopkeepers to sell to under 18s

- Everyday products give off gas or fumes – examples: glue, lighter fuel, many aerosol sprays containing everyday substances such as hairspray or deodorant, some paints, thinners and correcting fluids

- Effects: dizziness, giggling and dreaminess, hallucinations – last for 15 to 45 minutes; feeling of drowsiness; headache

- Other effects: nausea; blackouts; fatal heart problems; accidents when users not aware; suffocation; long-term damage to brain, liver and kidneys

- Risks: can cause death; when squirted down throat body produces fluid that floods lungs

Planning your work

Make a list of points you will include and the order in which you will use them. For example, you may want to begin with an explanation of solvents or you may choose to begin by explaining the dangers.

Tips for writing impersonal advice

- Write mainly in the present tense.
- Use formal vocabulary.
- Do not use the personal pronouns 'you' or 'I'.

16 Writing to analyse

This unit will help you to:

- ◆ **present ideas in a logical way**
- ◆ **think about different ways of organising and linking paragraphs**
- ◆ **use the passive voice to add a tone of formality**
- ◆ **use quotations and textual evidence when making judgements**
- ◆ **produce a formal essay within a specified time.**

Presenting ideas in a logical way

When you write to analyse you examine something closely and in detail. This could be a text, a series of events or a set of ideas. An important part of writing to analyse is drawing a conclusion based on your examination.

You write to analyse in a variety of subjects in school. For instance, in Geography you could be asked to analyse the impact tourism has had on a country. You write to analyse in History when you are asked to explain why events happened and the result of those events.

This text is a student's response to the following History task.

> *Why did the plague spread so quickly across Europe and what were the results?*

The annotations on the text show you how the student has organised his ideas and linked them together.

Topic sentence, introduces subject of paragraph.

Written in past tense.

Analysis begins here with explanation.

Topic sentence.

Phrase used to introduce further information.

Refers to people in general not individuals.

[The plague was transmitted to people by fleas which lived on rats.] In the 1330s China [was] one of the world's largest trading nations and therefore had links with many countries in Europe. The disease was carried by fleas and rats on ships and overland trading caravans travelling to Europe. In this way the disease spread very quickly throughout Europe.

The plague had long-lasting effects on life in Europe. [At that time medicine was unable to deal with this deadly disease and as a result many people died from it. After 5 years 25 million people were dead, one-third of Europe's people.] It caused serious labour shortages because so many people had died from it. Consequently, there were many riots as workers demanded and were refused higher wages.

[In addition,] the Church suffered. [People] had prayed for deliverance from the plague, yet their prayers were not answered. [So people began to question the Church and their belief in God.] So [it can be seen] the plague had a considerable effect on life in Europe.

Opening paragraph gives overview of the plague.

Gives detailed account of effects of plague.

Effects of the plague explained.

More effects explained.

Sentence uses passive voice to add formal tone to the conclusion.

Organising your ideas into paragraphs

When you are writing to analyse, it is very important to present your ideas logically so that readers can see how your ideas are developing.

Activity 1 ◈

One way of presenting your ideas clearly is to organise and link your paragraphs in a logical order. Answer these questions to help you understand how the writer of the text opposite has done this.

1 Look at the first sentence of paragraph 1. What is the purpose of the sentence?

2 Read the last sentence of paragraph 1 and the first sentence of paragraph 2. What is the word that links both of these?

3 Which phrase does the writer use to move on to new ideas at the beginning of paragraph 3?

4 How does the final sentence at the end of paragraph 3 link with the rest of the text?

Activity 2 ◈

1 You will notice that some of the words in the text have been highlighted in another colour. These are the connectives, words or phrases that 'glue' the text together and link the ideas. Using the right connectives helps you to organise an analysis logically. You will see that the connectives can be used in several positions in a sentence or a paragraph.
Make a list of the connectives in the text so that you can use them in your own writing. Put them under these headings:

Temporal connectives (these refer to time)

Causal connectives (which refer to the causes or effects)

Position in sentence or paragraph

2 Look at the final sentence where the **passive voice** has been used to give the conclusion a sense of authority and to make it more believable to readers. Using the passive voice also makes the text sound more formal.

Look again at the beginning of the last sentence: | *So it can be seen ...* |

Explain why this has more authority than a beginning like | *I think that ...* |

or | *You can see that ...* |

Rewrite the sentence starters in the box below to make them seem more formal. Look at the example to help you.

'You can see that' (**active voice**) changes to:
'It can be seen that' (**passive voice**).

In this case, the use of the second person pronoun 'you' is replaced by the impersonal 'it'. The verb 'can see' is changed to 'can be seen' making it passive.

| *I think that ...* |
| *Most people believe that ...* |

How to prepare for an analysis

Presenting ideas in a logical way is an important part of analysis. A good way to prepare a logical analysis is to make notes before you begin to write.

Activity 3 ⬧ICT

Study the information on this and be opposite page on the Fire of London, which took place in 1666. Use it to make brief notes to prepare for the following task:

> *Analyse the reasons why the Fire of London spread so quickly and why it caused so much damage.*

Think about how you will prepare your notes so that you can use them efficiently when you are ready for the writing task. Remember to include only the information you will need to prepare to do the task. Use the method below or devise your own.

◆ Use headings such as 'Streets', 'Buildings', 'Weather conditions', 'People' and 'Other causes' to group your ideas together. Remember that notes should be brief. Never write notes in full sentences.

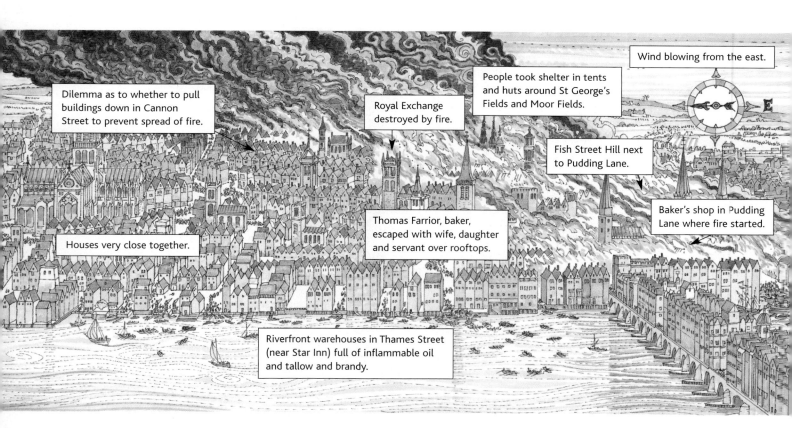

Fact file

◆ 80 per cent of the City of London destroyed
◆ 13,200 houses destroyed
◆ 90 parish churches destroyed
◆ 50 company halls destroyed
◆ Started 1 o'clock in the morning in baker's shop
◆ 1986: the Baker's Company offered a belated apology for the fire (320 years late)
◆ Began 2 September 1666
◆ Burned for five days
◆ Light from the fire could be seen 40 miles away
◆ Clouds of smoke stretched for nearly 50 miles

How to organise your notes

As you have seen, when you are writing to analyse it is important to present your ideas logically. It will help you to so this if you first arrange your notes in a sensible order so that you can then structure your paragraphs as you learned to do in Activity 1.

Activity 4 (WS)

Look at these notes made by a student on the Fire of London. They have been organised in random order. Help the student to organise these ideas by making a chart like the one below, then completing it. This will provide a logical order for the paragraphs in the analysis. You will have to combine several pieces of information in one paragraph. Aim to spend no more than five minutes on this activity.

Paragraph information I will include
1 How the fire began
2 How the fire developed
3 Conclusions about damage caused

date fire started

people who did not help

details of damage, number of houses destroyed etc.

fuel for fire: warehouses–oil, houses–roofs

weather conditions

length of time fire lasted

streets, narrow, full of rubbish, melting lead pouring down them

water wheel – London Bridge

Activity 5

With a partner look back at the work you have done so far in this unit. Re-read the model on page 154. Make a list of what you have learned so far about organising your ideas when writing to analyse.

Think about:

- ◆ how to prepare for an analysis
- ◆ how to organise your notes
- ◆ how to structure an analysis
- ◆ how to link ideas.

Activity 6

Using your notes on the Fire of London write your response to the following task:

> *Analyse the reasons why the Fire of London spread so quickly and why it caused so much damage.*

It may help you to organise your answer in this way:

Step 1: Number your notes in the order you want to use them.

Step 2: Divide your notes into paragraphs, grouping together all of the points on the same topic in one paragraph. Label your notes 'Paragraph 1', 'Paragraph 2' and so on, so that you can see how they will fit together.

Step 3: Write a first draft remembering to:
◆ write in the past tense
◆ begin with a general statement to introduce the topic to your readers
◆ use causal connectives to analyse the effects – for example, 'because', 'for this reason', 'as a result of', 'so'
◆ finish with a concluding statement to sum up the effects of the Fire of London.

Step 4: Revise your work asking yourself the following questions:
◆ Have I organised my work sensibly into paragraphs?
◆ Have I presented events in the best order for my analysis?
◆ Can I find at least three explanations of why damage was caused?
◆ Have I used the right connectives to link my ideas?
◆ Have I used connectives that explain cause and effect?
◆ Does my conclusion sum up for readers the reasons why the fire caused so much damage?
◆ If not, how will I change it?

Step 5: When you have made alterations to your work, write your final version.

Using quotations and evidence

The way you write an analysis changes depending on what is being analysed. When you analyse a text you need to examine the details of the text very closely and refer to them precisely. An effective way of doing this is to use quotations – that is, copying out the exact words used by the writer of the text.

Quotations are always written in inverted commas to show that you are using someone else's words. Once you have selected a quotation you make your own comment on it to explain why you have selected it.

Read the extract on page 160 from Samuel Pepys's Diary which gives a very personal account of the Fire of London.

An eye-witness account

2nd September

So near the fire as we could for smoke; and all over the Thames, with one's face in the wind you were almost burned with a shower of firedrops … as it grew darker [the fire] appeared more and more and in corners … as far as we could see up the hill of the City, in a most horrid **malicious** bloody flame, not like the flame of an ordinary fire.

… we saw the fire as only one entire arch of fire from this to the other side of the bridge … It made me weep to see it. The churches, houses, and all on fire and flaming at once, and a horrid noise the flames made, and the cracking of houses at their ruin.

… we were forced to begin to pack up our own goods and prepare for their removal.

3rd September

About 4 a-clock in the morning, my Lady Batten sent me a cart to carry away all my money and **plate** and best things to Sir W. Riders at Bednall Greene; which I did, riding myself in my nightgown in the cart … At night, lay down a little upon a quilt of W. Hewer in the office (all my own things being packed up or gone); and after me, my poor wife did the like – we having fed upon the remains of yesterday's dinner, having no fire nor dishes, nor any opportunity of dressing anything.

*from **Samuel Pepys's Diary***

Word bank
malicious – wanting to do harm
plate – gold and silver utensils and dishes

Look at this analysis of one part of the text.

Word used to introduce comment on quotation.

Samuel Pepys helps the reader to realise the effect the fire had [when he writes] 'you were almost burned with a shower of firedrops'. His use of the phrase 'a shower of firedrops' [suggests] there were so many sparks from the fire in the sky that walking beneath them was like being rained upon.

Phrase used to introduce quotation.

Comment based on evidence, quotation.

The analysis of the quotation is introduced by the word 'suggests'. Other useful words and phrases for introducing your analysis of quotations are:

◆ This shows …

◆ This makes the reader think …

◆ This tells the reader that …

◆ This implies …

◆ This emphasises …

Activity 7

Carefully re-read Pepys's diary entries opposite. Complete the following sentences by using suitable quotations from the diary. At the end of sentences 3, 4 and 5 you are also asked to comment on the quotations. Don't forget to put your quotations in inverted commas!

1 Samuel Pepys's diary makes it easy for the modern reader to understand how the Fire of London affected everyday life because he says _____ .

2 The detail that makes the reader feel sorry for Samuel Pepys and his wife is

    _____ .

3 Samuel Pepys describes the fire as _____ . His use of vocabulary such as _____ and _____ tells the reader that _____ .

4 Samuel Pepys writes about the fire: 'It made me weep to see it'. This shows that

    _____ .

5 When Pepys helps the reader to share his sensations of the fire by referring to the sounds he heard, he writes _____ . This section helps the reader to _____ .

Evaluating and making judgements

When you analyse texts you make judgements about them with evidence to support your view. This is different from expressing a purely personal opinion about a text such as 'I don't like this', or 'This poem doesn't interest me'.

Look at the poem below and the analysis that follows on page 163. The analysis was written by a student in answer to this examination question:

How well does the poet build up an atmosphere of tension in the poem?

Quiet

The night was so quiet
That the hum of the candle burning
Came to my ear,
A sound of breath drawn through a reed
5 Far off.

The night was so quiet
That the air in the room
Poised, waiting to crack
Like a straining
10 Stick.

The night was so quiet
That the blood and the flesh,
My visible self sunk in the chair,
Was a **power-house giant**, pulsing
15 Through the night.

Richard Church

> ### Word bank
> **power-house giant** – a huge store of energy

To answer the exam question, the student had to think about what it was asking her to do. She had to think about the meaning of the word 'tension'. She had to make her own judgements and evaluations about how well the writer had created tension. Before she started writing she made this plan.

Opening statement – refer to title of poem/theme of poem/remember to refer to tension

Technique	Evidence	Evaluation
repetition	repeats phrase 'night was so quiet'	effective, reminds reader of tense atmosphere
onomatopoeia	crack/hum	increases tension in atmosphere
quiet sounds/alliteration	self, sunk	
simile	like a straining stick	makes reader think silence will be broken
my final opinion	tension throughout poem	last stanza most effective

Activity 8 ICT

Read the first few paragraphs of the student's analysis below. As you read, answer the questions around the analysis to help you understand how the writer has structured her answer.

Opening statement. How does the writer refer to the title in this opening?

Word used to link ideas. What other words are used to link ideas?

Causal connective to comment on effect of words. Find two more of these.

Why has writer started new paragraph here?

[The poem has been written to put across to the reader that the poet enjoys the quietness of the night.] He [also] seems to find that the quiet causes tension as this builds up in the poem and is very clear at the end.

First, he has structured the poem [so that] the quietness is emphasised for the reader. He repeats the line 'The night was so quiet' at the beginning of every stanza. In this way the reader is reminded of the subject of the poem.

[In addition,] the poet has used quiet-sounding words such as 'hum' and 'breath' in order to suggest the quietness of the night. In the third stanza he uses alliteration with the words 'self' and 'sunk'. This is effective because it makes the poem quiet when it is read aloud because the 's' sound is a quiet one.

Writing tips for examination answers

- These are always written as formal essays.
- Use standard English, not slang.
- In general, write in the present tense.
- When you express your own opinion do not use the pronoun 'I'. Instead, use phrases like these for introducing your opinion: 'This is effective', and 'This helps the reader to understand …'.

Now read the following extract from a poem carefully. It has been labelled to show you the techniques the poet uses to build up an atmosphere of mystery and tension.

The Listeners

'Is there anybody there?' said the Traveller ———— Poem begins with question.

Knocking on the moonlit door; ———— Poem set at night time.

And his horse in the silence **champed** the grasses

Of the forest's ferny floor: ———— Alliteration creates soft gentle sounds.

5 And a bird flew up out of the turret,

Above the Traveller's head:

And he **smote** upon the door again a second time;

'Is there anybody there?' he said. ———— Question repeated, makes readers wonder what is going on.

But no one descended to the Traveller;

10 No head from the leaf-fringed sill ———— Word 'no' repeated to emphasise that he is alone.

Leaned over and looked into his grey eyes,

Where he stood **perplexed** and still ———— Build-up of soft quiet sounds creates ghostly atmosphere.

But only a host of phantom listeners ———— Reference to presence of ghosts.

That dwelt in the lone house then

15 Stood listening in the quiet of the moonlight

To that voice from the world of men: ... ———— Difference between Traveller and the Listeners brought out clearly.

Walter de la Mare

Word bank
champed – chewed
smote – banged hard
perplexed – puzzled

Activity 9 (WS) (ICT)

Answer this examination question on 'The Listeners':

> *How well does the poet build up an atmosphere of mystery and tension in the poem?*

It may help you to organise your answer in this way:

Step 1: Plan your answer paragraph by paragraph. Spend about 15 minutes on this section. Use these headings for your paragraphs:

◆ Introduction (brief comments on mystery and tension)

◆ Use of questions and repetition

◆ Use of soft-sounding words

◆ What the poet tells us about the 'Traveller' and the 'listeners'

◆ Conclusion to sum up comments on how the writer has created a mysterious atmosphere

Step 2: Number your paragraphs in the order you want to use them. Apart from the introduction and the conclusion you can choose your own order.

Step 3: Write your answer following these guidelines. Spend about 45 minutes on this section. Read 'Writing tips for examination answers' on page 163 before you begin.

◆ Begin with an opening statement that refers to the title of the question.

◆ Support your views by using quotations from the poem.

◆ Use causal connectives such as 'because' and 'as a result of' to show the effect of techniques.

◆ Link your ideas using phrases such as 'in addition to' and 'also'.

◆ End with a concluding statement to sum up how well the poet has built up an atmosphere of mystery and tension.

Step 4: As this is an examination answer, there will be a limited opportunity for redrafting and refining your work at the end.

◆ Read through each paragraph after you have written it and make your alterations before you move on.

◆ Save five minutes at the end of the test so that you can review your whole answer, adding anything you may have missed out and making any amendments.

Part 1
Writing to inform

Read these notes on the Blue Cross, an animal charity, and use them to write an information leaflet telling readers about the work that the charity does with animals. You should write three or four paragraphs. You could address your readers directly to make the information seem more personal.

Blue Cross founded in 1897
Aims: to help all animals
Promise: never to turn away an animal in need

- Leading animal welfare organisation
- New homes for animals
- Four animal hospitals and clinics
- Only funding: donations from public
- Caring for animals very expensive
- Jodie: starving puppy
- Free treatment for sick and injured animals
- Takes in homeless, unwanted animals
- Increase in number of animals needing help
- Eleven animal rescue centres
- No government funding
- Romany: 10 weeks old, abandoned kitten
- Zebedee: neglected horse
- Last year took in over 8,000 cats, dogs and horses

THE BLUE CROSS

Animal Welfare Charity

Step 1: Use the following headings to help you organise the notes from the list opposite.

Background information on the Blue Cross

Details of the work done by the organisation

Information about running costs and funding for the organisation

Step 2: Organise your ideas into three paragraphs.

Writing reminders

- ◆ Begin with a general statement to introduce the topic to your readers.
- ◆ Use the present tense to describe the work the organisation does now.
- ◆ Link your information with connectives such as 'also' and 'in addition'.
- ◆ Involve the reader by asking questions such as 'Did you know?'.
- ◆ Think about the ways you could present the information to make it clear for readers.
- ◆ How could you use headings and different fonts to make the information stand out?

Step 3: Check your work carefully and ask yourself these questions.

- ◆ Have I given enough information to my readers?
- ◆ Will they understand the work the Blue Cross does after reading my information leaflet?
- ◆ Have I linked my ideas clearly?
- ◆ How will my leaflet look to readers? Do I need to improve on the presentation?

Step 4: Make any alterations you think necessary, then write your final draft.

Part 2
Writing to explain

Many young people feel strongly about the way in which animals are treated. Choose a topic you feel strongly about and explain in detail why you feel this way. It may help to organise this task in the following way.

Step 1: Choose your topic – for example, cruelty to animals, bullying in schools, lack of facilities for young people in the area where you live.

Step 2: Make a list of the reasons why you feel strongly about your chosen topic. Number your reasons in the order in which you intend to write about them. Will you use your strongest reason first or save it to the end?

Step 3: Make a paragraph plan for your writing like this one.

Opening paragraph Introduce my topic to my readers, what I feel strongly about
Paragraph 2 My first set of reasons for feeling strongly about this
Paragraph 3 My next set of reasons
Paragraph 4 My conclusion, sum up my feelings

Writing reminders

◆ Write in the present tense.
◆ Use causal connectives to explain your feelings – for example, 'because', 'as a result of this', 'for this reason', 'in this way' and 'so'.
◆ Include evidence to support your explanations.

Step 4: Read through your work to check that your explanations and reasons come across clearly to your readers. Make any changes you think are necessary.

Step 5: Write the final draft.

Section E ◆ Speaking and listening ◈
Introduction

It's very easy to take speaking and listening for granted because they are things you do every day almost without thinking about them. But there are skills you can learn and develop.

Over the last two years of Key Stage 3 you will have been given the opportunity to speak and listen in a wide range of different contexts. You will have made presentations on your own. You will have worked in groups of different sizes and you will have used drama to explore ideas. The units in this section extend that range of contexts even further and present a wider range of skills to develop and situations to work in.

In Unit 18, *Making presentations*, you will explore how speech-makers use language in special ways to have an effect on their audience. You will learn how to develop your own ideas in spoken language.

In Unit 19, *Drama in speaking and listening*, you will look at how ideas have been explored in drama by playwrights before developing your own approach to an issue using dramatic techniques.

In Unit 20, *Working together*, you will focus on listening skills and working together on ideas using interview techniques.

Unit 21 tests you on the skills you will develop as you work carefully through the three units.

18 Making presentations

This unit will help you to:
- ◆ consider your abilities as a speaker in a range of situations
- ◆ use standard English to explain ideas
- ◆ identify the underlying themes of a talk
- ◆ analyse bias.

Thinking about speaking

Before you embark on the following series of activities in this unit, it is a good idea to think about your abilities as a speaker.

Activity 1 ⓦⓢ

1 In small groups of four or five, take turns to speak about the issues listed below. Use a frame like this one to make some notes before you discuss the issues with your group.

With what <u>kinds of people</u> am I most and least confident in conversation?	You might think about how you feel with family, friends, older people, strangers, those of the opposite sex and so on.	My notes:
In what <u>kinds of situations</u> am I most and least confident?	You might think about informal situations like chatting, being on the phone or face to face. You might also think about more formal situations like speaking in front of the class. What about being in a small group in class?	My notes:
Do I talk to my parents in a different style from the way I talk to friends?	Think about the kinds of words you use and whether you are more or less inhibited.	My notes:
Do I talk with friends differently in a small-group classroom discussion from the way I talk with them outside school?	Think about how much you contribute, how freely you speak, and whether there are different 'rules' for when and how you speak.	My notes:
Does my style of speech change when I stand at the front of the class to speak?	Think about the kind of language you use and your ability to speak confidently.	My notes:

2 When you have spent a few minutes speaking about these points and listening to each other, make some written notes about:

   a your strengths as a speaker and listener

   b what you would like to target for improvement.

Speaking in public

Some people have to become very confident and skilful public speakers. Before you look at how 'professional' speakers produce speeches you should try a little public speaking yourself.

Activity 2 will involve you in preparing a very short piece of public speaking. You will be talking about something that irritates you. Below is an example of someone talking about something that irritates them.

Man's best friend

'Now, man was created but man needed a companion, someone who would look after him, be his devoted servant, follow him wherever he went,
5   be loyal, faithful and obedient. And so dog was created. And because dog was such a mindless, chinless, tail-wagging, fawning creature, something with a bit of independence was created – cat.

10 How could anyone like dogs more than cats? I'll give you three reasons why dogs are a waste of space. One: they don't have minds of their own. They do whatever they're told. Two: they leave
15 piles of dog mess all over our streets. And three: they may love their owners but they're vicious to other people.

Remember a dog is for life, not just Christmas – yeah, a life sentence!'

◆   The speaker tries to attract attention at the opening of the speech by using a kind of biblical reference.
◆   There are two or three ideas in the main body of the speech explaining why the speaker doesn't like dogs.
◆   Then there's a conclusion based on a well-known slogan.

Activity 2

Give a 45-second talk to your class about something that really irritates you. Although this is quite a formal situation because it will be in front of the class, it does not require very formal language. You know your audience and they know you.

Step 1: Decide on a topic, a pet hate. It's always best to talk about things you actually know about and to express feelings you really have.

Step 2: Structure your talk. It may be brief, but it still requires:

◆ an opening in which you quickly grab the audience's attention and let them know what you're going to talk about
◆ a main body in which you give a couple of reasons or ideas to support your point
◆ a conclusion in which you leave the listeners with a memorable phrase.

Step 3: Deliver your speech. It is important to have eye contact with your audience, so you don't want to be reading a script. You need to decide whether you will prepare a script and learn it, or use prompt cards (for 45 seconds you will only need three or four prompts).

Example of prompts for speech on page 171

> – Now man was created ...
> – And so dog was created ...
> – How could anyone like dogs ... 1, 2, 3
> – Remember – life

Step 4: When you have delivered your speech and listened to other students in the class making theirs, write down your thoughts about:

◆ how good you feel what you said was (was it interesting for the audience?)
◆ how well you feel you expressed yourself   ◆ the benefits of planning.

Making speeches

Public speakers such as politicians often use speeches to try to persuade listeners of a particular point of view. Speeches are usually made in standard English rather than another dialect for at least one main reason: speeches are often intended to be heard by a whole nation, so it is important to use a form of language easily understood by all.

Can you think of other reasons?

In the early 1980s, Britain went to war with Argentina to recapture the Falkland Islands. For a long time, Argentina claimed ownership of the Falklands, and subsequently invaded them. Margaret Thatcher was the British Prime Minister at the time. When the conflict was over and British troops had regained the Falklands, she made an important speech, part of which is printed opposite. Follow the speech as it is read aloud by your teacher. As you listen, think about the 'message' of the speech and what you think the speaker's purpose is.

W
p.201

Speech to the nation

Today we meet in the aftermath of the **Falklands** Battle. Our country has won a great victory and we are entitled to be proud. This nation had the resolution to do what it knew had to be done – to do what it knew was right.

5 We fought to show that aggression does not pay, and that the robber cannot be allowed to get away with his swag. We fought with the support of so many throughout the world: the **Security Council**, the **Commonwealth**, the **European Community**, and the United States. Yet we also fought alone – for we fought for our own people and for our own **sovereign territory**.

Now that it is all over, things cannot be the same again, for we have learnt something
10 about ourselves – a lesson which we desperately needed to learn. When we started out, there were the waverers and the faint-hearts: the people who thought that Britain could no longer seize the **initiative** for herself; the people who thought we could no longer do the great things which we once did; and those who believed that our decline was irreversible – that we could never again be what we were. There were those who would not admit it –
15 even perhaps some here today – people who would have strenuously denied the suggestion but – in their heart of hearts – they too had their secret fears that it was true: that Britain was no longer the nation that had built an Empire and ruled a quarter of the world.

Well, they were wrong. The lesson of the Falklands is that Britain has not changed and that this nation still has those **sterling** qualities which shine through our history. This
20 generation can match their fathers and grandfathers in ability, in courage, and in resolution. We have not changed. When the demands of war and the dangers
25 to our own people call us to arms – then we British are as we have always been – competent, courageous and resolute.

Margaret Thatcher

Word bank

Falklands – small islands off Argentina
Security Council – the most powerful countries in the United Nations
Commonwealth – collection of states, once part of the British Empire
European Community – an earlier version of the European Union
sovereign territory – power to rule the country
initiative – opportunity
sterling – admirable and powerful

Activity 3 (ws)

In groups of four or five, discuss the following five areas. One member of each group should make notes (based on the chart below) that could be used for a brief feedback to the rest of the class on the group's conclusions.

The issue for discussion	Some ideas to discuss	Notes
1 The **structure** of the speech	There are four paragraphs. Label each one with a sub-heading that will sum it up.	
2 The **speaker's point of view** or **perspective**	Think about: ◆ the attitude towards Argentina and the kinds of words the speaker uses to describe that country ◆ the attitude towards people who disagreed with the war ◆ whether the speech was based on facts or opinions.	
3 The **audience**	◆ The speaker's use of 'we' and 'they', and the absence of 'I'. ◆ Does the speaker think her audience shares her beliefs?	
4 The **language**	◆ Is the language used similar to yours or are there words and expressions you would not use in ordinary speech? ◆ Does the speaker use any slang or does she shorten words as people do when they are in conversation? ◆ On one occasion the speaker does use some slang: she uses the word 'swag', a slang term for things that have been stolen. Why do you think she uses it? ◆ Is the speech organised into proper sentences? How simple or complex are they?	
5 The **purpose**	Is the speaker's purpose to inform? Persuade? Entertain? Celebrate? Argue?	

Bias

If you look at an issue from only one side then there is bias. Bias emerges if certain things are neglected or altered in order to make a point. For example, in the speech by Mrs Thatcher on page 173, the following statement is made: 'Our country has won a great victory'. Who might look at this statement and disagree?

Activity 4

1 What has been omitted from the following statement that you might want to know before you agreed with it?

We fought with the support of so many throughout the world.

2 Look back to Mrs Thatcher's speech on page 173. Find three examples of her use of words that show the speech has a clear bias to it.

3 In Activity 2 you made a 45-second speech. You have also explored quite a famous historical speech. What do you think you can learn from the 'famous' speech that could help you to become a better public speaker? Share ideas in your small group.

Looking at language and structure

Now look at the following very different speech. This speech was made by Sojourner Truth in 1851. She was a former slave in America who became very active in the anti-slavery movement. The speech, like Mrs Thatcher's, was made to an audience of mainly women.

Activity 5 ⓦⓢ

1 Listen to the speech as it is read aloud by your teacher and as you do, think about the following question:

> In what ways is the vocabulary and expression of this speech different from the previous speech?

You should consider: ◆ the vocabulary she uses ◆ her use of repetition.

And a'n't I a woman?

Dat man ober dar say dat womin needs to be helped into carriages, and lifted over ditches, and to hab de best place everywhar. Nobody eber helps me into carriages, or ober mud-puddles, or gibs me any best place. And a'n't I a woman? Look at me! Look at my arm! I have ploughed and planted, and gathered into barns, and no man could head me! And a'n't I a woman? I could work as much and eat as much as a man – when I could get it – and bear de lash as well! And a'n't I a woman? I have borne thirteen childern, and see 'em mos' all sold off to slavery, and when I cried out with my mother's grief, none but Jesus heard me! And a'n't I a woman?

Den dey talks 'bout dis ting in de head; what dis dey call it? (Intellect, whispered someone near.) Dat's it, honey. What's dat go to do wid womin's right o nigger's rights? If my cup won't hold but a pint, and yourn holds a quart, wouldn't ye be mean not to let me have my little half-measure full?

Den dat little man in black dar, he say women can't have as much rights as man, 'cause Christ wan't a woman. Whar did your Christ come from? From God and a woman! Man had nothin' to do wid Him.

Sojourner Truth

2 In your group discuss your thoughts on the two discussion points.

3 Use the scripts of the two speeches and consider the following to help you prepare brief notes on the similarities and differences in the language and structure in the two speeches:

   a Does this speech seem more or less organised and structured than Mrs Thatcher's?

   b What evidence is there that this speech is being improvised, that it is 'impromptu' i.e. she is making it up as she speaks? What evidence is there, however, that the speech is planned?

4 Using your notes, prepare a brief feedback to the rest of the class in which you outline similarities and differences between the two speeches. Talk about:

   ◆ Obvious differences in language and expression. Can you explain the differences?

   ◆ Structure. Are both speeches as clearly organised into sections?

   ◆ The point of view about the subject. Are the two speeches based on facts or opinions? Does each speaker assume the audience shares her point of view?

Activity 6

In her speech, Sojourner Truth repeated the phrase 'And a'n't I a woman?' four times.

1 What do you think she meant by those words? Look carefully at the four places it appears in the speech and think about whether they mean the same thing each time she uses them.

2 Write down (in note form) what you think the words mean.

Activity 7

Use what you have learned in this unit to prepare and deliver a formal speech lasting about one minute, based on the idea:

> The kind of world you would like to see in the future.

Because it is a formal speech it will probably be delivered in standard English without the use of slang or dialect words, unless you deliberately use them for effect.

Activity 8

You may have heard of Martin Luther King and his famous 'I have a Dream' speech in which he talked about his hopes for the future using the phrase 'I have a dream today'.

Step 1: Brainstorm some ideas. Spend some time thinking about the kinds of ideas you would like to express.

◆ What kinds of things do you feel are wrong in the world?

◆ Is there one main thing you would like to talk about or are there several?

Step 2: Consider a structure for your speech. The two speeches you have seen leading up to this activity are paragraphed – broken down into separate sections. Here are some suggestions for a framework.

- ◆ You could take the idea of 'I have a dream' and use that phrase.
- ◆ You could work with a partner on a 'We have a dream' speech in which you each take sections.
- ◆ You could try to come up with your own memorable repeated phrase. Something like 'The world will be a better place ...' or something deliberately informal used for effects, like 'Ain't that good?'.

Step 3: Script your speech. Your speech should last for at least a minute. It would be best to have a full written version of this speech in front of you, but it would be best of all if you had learned some of it off by heart.

Step 4: Deliver your speech. As you deliver your speech it is very important to establish eye contact with your audience. Pay attention to the pace of your speech, and which words or phrases you will emphasise.

Step 5: Listen carefully to each other's speeches. Pay particular attention to those made by the members of your small group. Listen for evidence that they have used some of the ideas for effective speech-making that you have worked on in this unit.

Step 6: Evaluate your speeches. When you have all delivered your speeches, work in your small group and give feedback to each other about how effective the speeches have been. What were the strengths and in what ways could they be improved? Focus on:

- ◆ language – was the speech delivered in standard English?
- ◆ structure – was there a clear opening, main body and conclusion of your speech?
- ◆ relationship with audience – did the speech 'engage' the audience?

This unit will help you to:
- develop and compare different interpretations of dramatic scenes
- convey action, character and atmosphere when performing scenes
- use dramatic techniques to explore ideas
- consider the range of dramatic techniques that can be used.

Blood Brothers

Blood Brothers is a musical play by Willy Russell. It is about twin boys, Eddie and Mickey, who are separated at birth. Their mother, Mrs Johnston, is a cleaner who struggles financially to make ends meet. A rich woman, Mrs Lyons, persuades Mrs Johnston to hand over one of the twins and takes Eddie. The two boys grow up in the same area but in two very different households. They meet without realising how they are related and, at the age of eight, become best friends and 'blood brothers'.

Below is Act 2 Scene 9 from the play. Mrs Lyons has decided to move to a new district so that Eddie won't meet Mickey any more.

Work in small groups of four or five. Two of each group should read the parts of Mrs Lyons and Eddie. Read it through fairly quickly before looking at the activities that follow it.

Act 2 Scene 9

Birdsong. **The Mother** [Mrs Johnston] *watches them for a moment before she exits.*

	Mrs Lyons	Well Edward, do you like it here?
	Eddie	(*unenthusiastic*) It's very nice.
5	**Mrs Lyons**	(*bending and pointing*) Look Edward … look at those cows … and those trees. Oh Edward, you're going to like it so much out here, aren't you?
	Eddie	Yes. Are you feeling better now, Mummy?
10	**Mrs Lyons**	Much better darling. Oh look, Edward … look, look at those birds … look at that lovely black and white one …
	Eddie	(*immediately covering his eyes*) Don't Mummy, don't … don't look …

15	**Mrs Lyons**	Edward!
	Eddie	It's a magpie. Never look at one magpie. It's one for sorrow.
	Mrs Lyons	Edward, that's just a silly superstition.
	Eddie	It's not, it's not, Mickey told … me …
	Mrs Lyons	Edward, I think we can forget the silly things that Mickey says.
20	**Eddie**	I'm going inside, I want to read.
	Mrs Lyons	Edward, children take time to adapt to new surroundings. But you soon won't even remember that you once lived somewhere else. In a few weeks you'll forget him – Mickey. (*She smiles at him and nods. They stand together for a moment, surveying the land before them.*)
25	**Eddie**	What's that Mummy?
	Mrs Lyons	(*craning to see*) What?
	Eddie	There … look … below the hill.
	Mrs Lyons	What? Oh those houses? That's the beginning of a council estate. But we've arranged with the gardener, he's going to plant a row of poplars
30		down at the end of the paddock there. Once they're in we won't even be able to see that estate. Oh, I love it out here. I feel secure here. I feel warm and safe. Once the trees are planted we won't even see that estate. (*She beams a smile at him as they turn and head for the house.*)

*from **Blood Brothers** by Willy Russell*

Activity 1

You are going to interpret the character of Mrs Lyons. In your groups, explore whether Mrs Lyons is a caring, sympathetic character or whether she is snobbish and unsympathetic.

1 **Her accent and vocabulary.** Look first of all at her speeches in Act 2 Scene 9. Then discuss whether there are two different ways they could be spoken.

   a Does she use any vocabulary that suggests she might speak with a 'posh' accent?

   b Are there places where her vocabulary is 'ordinary'?

   c What is your opinion? Should she speak with a 'posh' accent or not?

2 **Her relationship with Eddie.** What is it like?

   a Are there any places in the text where she could be almost ignoring what he says and just talking about what she wants to?

   b Are there places where she could be said to be paying a lot of attention to what Eddie is saying?

3 **Eddie's reactions to her.**

   a What does Eddie say that could be emphasised to show the mother as not a very sympathetic character?

   b Alternatively, what does he say that could be used to draw attention to her being a caring, loving mother?

Acting the part of Mrs Lyons

In Act 2 Scene 9 of *Blood Brothers* (pages 178–179), the playwright includes some stage directions for the actors. In other places, how the actors behave has to be *interpreted* by them.

If you wanted Mrs Lyons to be a caring sympathetic character when she says 'Edward!' after he has said 'Don't look', you could put in a stage direction that says: *puts her arm around him, concerned.*

If you wanted her to be seen as less sympathetic you could insert the following direction: *glaring at him, reprimanding him.*

Activity 2

1 What stage direction could you use to help the audience feel sympathy for Mrs Lyons when Edward says: 'I want to read'?

2 How could you change that direction to make her seem less sympathetic?

3 When you have discussed these points in your groups, prepare two different readings of this scene.

   ◆ Two in each group should read the scene as though Mrs Lyons is a caring and sympathetic character.

   ◆ Then two different members of each group should read it in a different way so that she seems more snobbish, less sympathetic.

4 When you have read the scene in these two different ways, discuss which version:

   a seems to fit the evidence of the text best

   b is the most entertaining.

5 Choose one of your versions to read aloud to the class. When you have finished, your 'audience' should be able to tell you whether your version was the sympathetic or unsympathetic one and how they knew.

Activity 3 ⓦⓢ

As each version of the scene is read, think about the ways in which the second one is similar to, but also different from, the first one. You should think about similarities and differences in:

   ◆ the situation
   ◆ the mother's behaviour
   ◆ the mother/son relationship
   ◆ the characters' speech.

Mickey and The Mother

Remain in your small groups and read the next scene of *Blood Brothers* (opposite). There are two characters: The Mother and Mickey. A couple of years after Mrs Lyons and Eddie moved to be away from Mrs Johnston and Mickey, Mrs Johnston is being re-housed to the council estate close to where Mrs Lyons lives.

Act 2 Scene 10

As they exit we see **Mickey** *and* **The Mother** *enter, each carrying a suitcase.* **The Mother** *is vigorously taking in the fresh air and leading the way as* **Mickey** *struggles with the case. He is now twelve.*

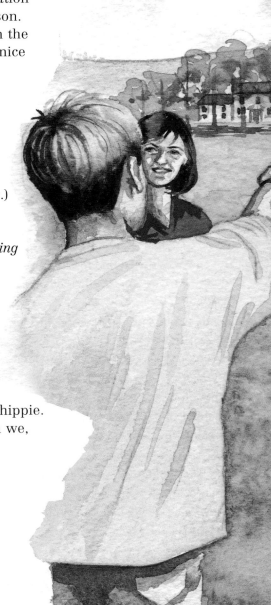

Mickey	(*stopping and pointing*) Is that our new house there Mam?
5 **The Mother**	(*looking*) Where?
Mickey	There … look, you can just see it behind that row of trees.
The Mother	(*laughing*) Mickey … give over will you. The Corporation don't build houses like that. That's a private house son. (*She points in the other direction.*) No … look, down the hill … that's where ours is. Look. Oh … son, isn't it nice out here eh? Eh?
Mickey	It's like the country isn't it, Mam?
The Mother	Eh, we'll be all right here, son. Away from the muck and dirt. And the bloody trouble. You can breathe out here, Mickey. Hey, I could dance. Couldn't you?
Mickey	(*alarmed*) What?
The Mother	(*grabbing him*) Come on … (*She lilts the tune and waltzes him around the road as he protests vigorously.*)
Mickey	Mother … Mother put me down will you. (*Breaking away, leaving his mother to dance alone, looking around and checking that nobody saw him then watching his mother as she dances. Slowly a huge smile breaking across his face.*)
The Mother	And what are you laughing at? I used to be a good dancer you know. A very good dancer in fact.
Mickey	I'm not laughing. I'm smiling. I haven't seen you happy like this for ages.
The Mother	Well I'm happy now. You never know, Mickey, play your cards right, we might have tea from the chippie.
Mickey	(*picking up his case, as does* **The Mother**) Ooh, can we, Mam, can we?
The Mother	Come on, come on. Hey, Jesus, where's the others? Where's our Sammy and the others?
35 **Mickey**	They went into that field, Mam.
The Mother	Which field?
Mickey	(*pointing*) That field.
The Mother	(*craning, horror-stricken, shouting*) Sammy, Sammy get off that cow before I bleedin' kill you. Oh Jeez, what's our Donna Marie put her sodding foot in? Sammy, get hold of her … wipe it off … oh … come on, Mickey … come on … (*Exit*).

from **Blood Brothers** *by Willy Russell*

Activity 4

1 Look at the similarities between Scenes 9 and 10. Discuss what is *similar* in:

    a the situation

    b the mother/son relationship

    c the behaviour of the mother.

2 Look at the differences between the scenes. Discuss what is *different* in:

    a the language of the characters

    b the action.

Preparing both scenes

Often, different directors have different ideas about how a scene should be acted. Look at the examples of Director 1 and Director 2 below, who are both working on Act 2 Scenes 9 and 10 of *Blood Brothers*.

Director 1

Director 1 would like to emphasise the similarities between the two scenes and the two pairs of characters. She wants the scene to be played with the following in mind.

◆ The audience are to find Mrs Lyons and Mrs Johnston equally sympathetic. Both are loving, caring mothers making the best of things.

◆ She doesn't want the obvious differences between the two to be exaggerated. (This will be achieved by considering such things as actions, body language and tone of voice.)

◆ Although one pair is poor and the other rich – that shouldn't be hidden – she would like the audience to realise the connections between the two scenes.

◆ She wonders if Eddie and Mickey, even if they have different feelings about moving house, could do similar things to show they are the same age. (They could be given some similar action, clothing or stage prop.)

◆ She feels the same might be possible with the two mothers – both should be presented as caring. (This could be achieved by some similar action.)

Director 2

Director 2 would like the differences between the two families to be highlighted. He wants the following differences to be emphasised.

◆ The difference in social class – rich/poor, posh/down to earth. (This could be done through emphasising accent and vocabulary differences and different kinds of actions.)

◆ The difference between the two mothers. Mrs Johnston is the 'real' mother and the audience is to be attracted to her, whereas Mrs Lyons is a 'false' mother and the audience is to find her unsympathetic and snobbish.

◆ Similarly, Eddie is to be seen as rather babyish because of the influence of Mrs Lyons, whereas Mickey is a more likeable, independent character.

Activity 5

In your small groups, decide which director's view you wish to adopt. Then prepare a reading of the two scenes, which reflects what that director wants.

Acting the scenes

Actions can completely change the meanings of words. For example, at the beginning of Act 2 Scene 9, Mrs Lyons asks Eddie if he is going to enjoy it in their new house and he answers, 'Yes.' If he smiles at her genuinely when he says it, it will mean 'Yes'. But if his back is turned towards her and the audience sees that he says it through clenched teeth, then it would mean 'No'.

Activity 6

1 When you have read through Act 2 Scenes 9 and 10 in a way that is appropriate, you should explore the actions of the characters. What should each character do:
   a when they speak?
   b when the other character is speaking?

2 As two of you read the parts, the others in each group should act as directors, advising the two 'actors' about what they could be doing as they speak and respond.

3 Rehearse your two scenes, then show them to the rest of the class.

4 As you watch the performances of other groups, jot down brief notes about how effectively they:
   a deliver their words to draw out differences between characters
   b use actions to draw attention to similarities and differences between the characters.

Activity 7

When you have shown your own interpretation of Act 2 Scenes 9 and 10, and watched others perform their versions, write a short piece about the version you felt was best. You should write about the following.

1 Your opinion of the writer's skill. Were the scenes interesting? Entertaining? Did the writer use dialogue that was convincingly real? Did he show differences between the different characters?

2 The performance you liked best of the ones you watched. Explain why you felt one was better than the others. You should think about how good the acting was and whether it was easy to tell which of the two directors' ideas the actors were following.

Producing your own drama texts

Blood Brothers explores, among other things, the differences between rich and poor. Dramatists and novelists often write about social issues like this. Below is an extract from the novel *Stone Cold* by Robert Swindells, which describes what it is like to sleep rough. The narrator is a teenager. Read the extract and think about the issues it raises for your task in Activity 8.

Stone Cold

So you pick your spot. Wherever it is (unless you're in a squat or a derelict house or something) it's going to have a floor of stone, tile, concrete or brick. In other words it's going to be hard and cold. It might be a bit cramped too – shop doorways often are. And remember, if it's winter you're going to be half frozen before you even start.

5   Anyway you've got your place, and if you're lucky enough to have a sleeping-bag you unroll it and get in.

Settled for the night? Well maybe, maybe not. Remember my first night? The Scouser? 'Course you do. He kicked me out of my bedroom and pinched my watch. Well, that sort of thing can happen any night, and there are worse things. You could be peed

10   on by a drunk or a dog. Happens all the time – one man's bedroom is another man's lavatory. You might be spotted by a gang of lager louts on the look-out for someone to maim. That happens all the time too, and if they get carried away you can end up dead. There are the guys who like young boys, who think because you're a dosser you'll do anything for dosh, and there's the **psycho** who'll knife you for your pack.

15   So, you lie listening. You bet you do. Footsteps. Voices. Breathing, even. Doesn't help you sleep.

Then there's your bruises. What bruises? Try lying on a stone floor for half an hour. Just half an hour. You can choose any position you fancy, and you can change position as often as you like. You won't find it comfy, I can tell you. You won't sleep unless

20   you're dead drunk or **zonked on downers**. And if you are, and do, you're going to wake up with bruises on hips, shoulders, elbows, ankles and knees – especially if you're a bit thin from not eating properly. And if you do that six hours a night for six nights you'll feel like you fell out of a train. Try sleeping on concrete then.

And don't forget the cold. If you've ever tried dropping off to sleep with cold feet,

25   even in bed, you'll know it's impossible. You've got to warm up those feet, or lie awake. And in January, in a doorway, in wet trainers, it can be quite a struggle. And if you manage it, chances are you'll need to get up for a pee, and then it starts all over again.

And those are only some of the hassles. I haven't mentioned stomach cramps

30   from hunger, headaches from the flu, toothache, fleas and lice. I haven't talked about homesickness, depression or despair. I haven't gone into how it feels to want a girl-friend when your circumstances make it virtually impossible for you to get one – how it feels to know you're a social outcast in fact, a non-

35   person to whom every ordinary everyday activity is closed.

*from **Stone Cold** by Robert Swindells*

Word bank
psycho – mentally unstable person
zonked on downers – under the effect of drugs

Theatre in education performance

'Theatre in education' is a term used to describe theatre companies who go into schools and use drama to explore issues with students because they believe that drama is a more effective way of educating young people than lecturing them.

Activity 8 (ws)

You are going to work in small groups to produce a 'theatre in education' performance lasting between five and ten minutes. First of all, study the background information. Use the outline below to plan and produce your performance.

1 **Background information to your performance**

Your performance is for young teenagers. It is about the issue of young people and homelessness. There are two main dramatic techniques you are to use to explore the issue: **a** inventing short scenes to act out (like the kinds of scenes you looked at in *Blood Brothers*); **b** using characters in role to talk directly to the audience about their imagined experiences.

Your performance should be a mixture of the two. It is recommended that you move between the two by 'freezing' the action of a scene, then having one character step out to talk to the audience.

The performance should highlight the different reasons young people become homeless, reveal the problems and dangers young people face on the streets, and offer guidance and advice.

To help you with these points, some of the main messages to be promoted are listed below. Your main task is to think about how to bring these issues to life through drama.

> **Some reasons for young people becoming homeless**
> - Abuse   - Arguments about money and behaviour
> - Marriage break-ups and the arrival of new partners   - Drugs
>
> **Some of the problems and dangers faced by homeless young people**
> - Lack of hygiene and comfort   - Increased risk of violence
> - Inability to make relationships   - The feeling of being an outcast
> - Inability to get work because of the lack of a permanent address
>
> **Guidance and advice**
> - It's far better to deal with the problems at home than it is to deal with problems on the street.
> - To seek help before making the decision to leave home.
> - Talk to friends.   - Use the free phone lines on offer – for example, Childline.

2 **Your approach**

a Try to keep it simple. Avoid a complicated drama. Plan your drama by making a chart like the one on page 186.

Approach	Your notes
Decide on a 'story' and how many characters you will need.	*Our story will be about:*
Now think about your performance. In your small groups you may have to play many different parts. Characters you create need to be different and need to speak in different ways. Think of how you could vary language according to the character. Remember the work you did on the language of the characters in *Blood Brothers*. You could use: ◆ slang and colloquial speech for the young homeless person ◆ a more standard speech for, say, any parents involved ◆ particular terms for any professionals you create – for example, a police officer might use vocabulary such as 'assault', 'caution', 'trespass' and 'the rights of shopkeepers'.	Use this section for notes about the different parts

b When you have discussed these issues you should prepare a plan for the sequence of scenes.

c Rehearse your ideas before showing your performance to the rest of the class.

3 After the performance

When you have performed and watched others present their dramas, discuss:

a What have we learned?:

b If we were to start again, what could we do differently?

This unit will help you to:
- listen carefully and consider the kinds of skills that aid listening
- consider the needs of listeners
- contribute to work in a small group
- develop interviewing skills.

Developing listening skills

Listening to a long talk can be difficult for many reasons:

- it's hard to concentrate
- you don't like what is being said
- the talk is hard to understand
- the tone of voice is monotonous or the content repetitive.

Listening for particular information

When you are reading for information you sometimes *skim* a piece of text to get the gist of it. At other times you might be looking for a particular piece of information. In those circumstances you *scan* the text and pay little attention to what you don't need.

Activity 1

Below are two lists of words, A and B.

List A:	apple	red	John	Maggie	pear	mouse	Yvette
	screen	blue	Leon	grape	keyboard	Michelle	purple
	banana	Tony	peach	Donna	software	green	Frank
	brown	Mike	Katy	hard disk			
List B:	Maths	chair	scarf	ice-cream	rugby	swimming	hockey
	shoes	chips	RE	table	orange	Science	
	wardrobe	hat	French	netball	sausages	socks	
	Art	bed	rice	sofa	sweatshirt	basketball	

- In list A there are some fruits, colours, boys' names, girls' names and things to do with computers.
- In list B there are some pieces of furniture, school subjects, clothes, things to eat and some sports.

1 Working in pairs, choose a list. One of you will listen, while one of you reads. The listener should not be able to see the list. The reader should tell the partner which things to listen for – for example, fruits only.

2 The reader reads the whole list aloud. Then the listener recounts the items s/he has been told to listen for.

3 To make it more difficult, the reader could ask the listener to listen for two categories.

Listening and making notes

Sometimes it is helpful to write things down when you are listening to a talk. It's useful to use abbreviations when you are making notes. For example, instead of writing down:

◆ 'Thursday', you could simply write 'Thurs' or even 'Th'.

If you are used to sending text messages on a mobile phone you will be aware of abbreviations that you can use. For example, a single letter 'u' instead of the word 'you' can be very useful when you are quickly making notes and trying to listen to a speaker at the same time. Text messaging often misses out vowels, but the words are still readable. For example, you should be able to interpret the following:

Lstnng + mkng nts

You need to make sure that you can recognise the abbreviations later on. For example, if you were using first and last letters of words for abbreviations you might use 'Ty' for a day of the week, but then not be sure later if you meant 'Tuesday' or 'Thursday'.

Activity 2 (ws)

Below and on pages 189–190 are two eye-witness accounts. Working in pairs, one of you should read out loud from the first account, while the other makes notes. Then swap roles for the second eye-witness account. On each occasion, the listener should have his or her book closed.
Steps 1 to 6 will help you to work through this activity.

Step 1: Before the reader reads out the first eye-witness account, s/he should say to the listener:

I am going to read you a story told by an eye-witness. I want you to listen carefully and make any notes you think will be useful. When I am finished I am going to ask you to tell me:

- ◆ *what happened*
- ◆ *who was involved*
- ◆ *where and when it happened*
- ◆ *why it happened.*

Before I begin you might want to put those sub-headings down on your piece of paper.

Eye-witness account 1

'My name is Bob Elliott. I'm not really involved in this story, I just saw it. It was last Thursday. I'd just finished work – I work at Dixons on the main street in Stockport. It's on the corner by the traffic lights near the Town Hall. It must have been about five o'clock.

'I was just coming out the front door when I heard this screech of brakes. I looked up and saw this car – it was bright red, a Ford Mondeo I thought. It had screeched to a halt outside the pizza place opposite the Town Hall. A young man jumped out of the driver's seat and stopped the car behind him – it was a small green car. I'm not sure what make it was. The driver of the red Ford looked furious: he was shouting and swearing at the green car.

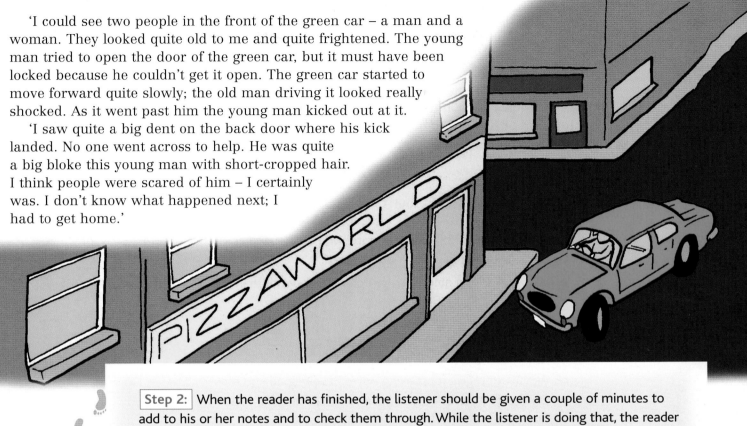

'I could see two people in the front of the green car – a man and a woman. They looked quite old to me and quite frightened. The young man tried to open the door of the green car, but it must have been locked because he couldn't get it open. The green car started to move forward quite slowly; the old man driving it looked really shocked. As it went past him the young man kicked out at it.

'I saw quite a big dent on the back door where his kick landed. No one went across to help. He was quite a big bloke this young man with short-cropped hair. I think people were scared of him – I certainly was. I don't know what happened next; I had to get home.'

Step 2: When the reader has finished, the listener should be given a couple of minutes to add to his or her notes and to check them through. While the listener is doing that, the reader should make a list of the important information from the story under the headings:

◆ What? ◆ Where? ◆ When? ◆ Who? ◆ Why?

Step 3: The listener should tell as much of the story back in as much detail as possible, while the partner checks off details.

Step 4: The reader and listener should swap roles and do the whole exercise again with Account 2 below. The reader should explain to the listener what to do (as in Step 1), then read the story below.

Eye-witness account 2

'This happened outside the school gates at Hope Comprehensive, the big school on Sutton Avenue in Coventry. It was a Tuesday, not last Tuesday but the one before – the 3rd of October.

'I was waiting to pick up my daughter, Anna. I was parked about fifty yards from the school gate, back outside the newsagent's – Quickshop I think it's called. I heard the bell go so it must have been 3.15.

'There was quite a lot of traffic about, there usually is at that time of day. The first lot of kids had crossed at the pelican crossing and I was looking for Anna when I saw a car travelling down the road in my direction. I noticed it because it was travelling fast, much faster than you should on that road.

'Then I saw the boy come running out of the school. He was obviously going to run across the pelican crossing while the amber lights were flashing. The driver of the speeding car saw him at about the same time and slammed on his brakes. There was a terrible screeching of brakes before he skidded on to the pavement and into the wall.

'I got out of my car and went forward to help. The boy was shaken but unhurt. He's in Anna's class and his name is Pete Neale. The driver of the car – it was some kind of Fiat, a red one – was also unhurt, but seemed to be in some kind of shock. I phoned the emergency services on my mobile.

Step 5: Repeat Steps 2 and 3.

Step 6: Compare the kinds of notes you each made as you listened. Are they similar? Compare the strategies each of you used.

◆ Was one of you able to write down more detail than the other?
◆ How was that possible?
◆ What kinds of abbreviations did you use?
◆ Did you write your notes horizontally or vertically?
◆ How did you try to fix the *sequence* of events in your notes?
◆ Which strategies for making notes have helped you most?
◆ On the next occasion you have to listen for information what could you do that will make you a more effective listener?

Giving talks

Listening can be quite a difficult activity. As well as listeners trying to be active and using strategies like note-taking to help themselves, it is important for speakers to organise talks in ways that make listening easier for an audience.

Many people can get nervous at the thought of giving a talk to an audience. It's a perfectly normal response. In fact, being a little nervous is probably a good thing because it might help reinforce the importance of good planning. There are things you can do to make it easier and that will contribute to a successful talk.

◆ Be well prepared.
◆ Know what you want to talk about and avoid 'fillers' such as 'erm,' and 'you know'.
◆ Try to look confident.
◆ Try to control your breathing.
◆ Don't fidget with anything.
◆ Try to vary your voice and facial expressions.
◆ Think about gestures you could use to reinforce a point.

One of the most important things is to try to make eye contact with your audience.

Activity 3 (ws)

1 Working with a partner, prepare a simple talk entitled 'Five people I'd really like to meet'. Your talk will basically be a list with some reasons attached. For example, you might begin:

> 'The first person I'd really like to meet is the Prime Minister. I'd like to ask him what it's like to be so famous. Another person I'd like to meet is …'

2 Deliver your talk to your partner while looking into his or her eyes – across a desk, for example.

3 Now stand on your own at the front of the class and talk for about 30 seconds on anything you want. Make it simple. It might be something like 'How to make a cup of tea', or 'What I've done today'. As you talk, look at everyone in the room at least once. You will find that you need to talk quite slowly.

4 Audience: you should cross your fingers at the start of the speech. When the speaker catches your eye, uncross them. At the end of the talk let the speaker know how many fingers are still crossed.

Speaking clearly and avoiding 'fillers'

It is very important to speak clearly when talking to an audience. Everyone needs to be able to hear you, so it is important not to mumble or talk too quickly.

'Fillers' are sounds like 'um', 'erm', 'uh', 'you know', and 'like'. We all use them. They are sounds we use to fill in little silences while we are thinking. They are perfectly acceptable in conversation and discussion when you are thinking aloud. If you use them a lot in *prepared* talks it sounds like you are not too sure of what you want to say.

Using prompts may help you to avoid using 'fillers'. Prompts are a list of the different things you might say. They help you work out an order to your talk. For example, some prompts on 'My favourite television programmes' might look like this.

> ◆ I like soaps.   ◆ EastEnders is my favourite.
> ◆ The characters are really good …   ◆ I also like Family Affairs.
> ◆ It's good because …

Activity 4

Working in groups of between four and six, you are each going to talk for one minute on a subject that you have chosen from the list below:

◆ My favourite television programmes. ◆ My taste in music.

◆ How I'd spend £1 million. ◆ A special interest of mine.

1 When you have chosen your subject, spend five minutes working out what you are going to say. *Don't* write out a script. But you might find it helpful to write out some prompts.

2 Each group member has to deliver his or her talk without using any 'fillers'. Each member also has to make eye contact with everyone in the group.

3 The rest of the group should make a note of how many 'fillers' are used and whether they feel the speaker made eye contact.

4 When each person has given their talk, discuss among yourselves how well they all managed to avoid 'fillers'.

Speaking at interviews

Speeches are often made on important occasions. There are other occasions when your ability to speak well is particularly important.

Interviews are occasions when people are judged.

Because of your age, you may never have experienced an interview. However, you will almost certainly know something about them and will experience them when you are interviewed for your Work Experience placement, for example.

People at interviews need to sound confident. The following things may help with this.

◆ Spend some time before the interview thinking about which qualities the job requires so that you are prepared.

◆ Establish eye contact with the interview panel and be enthusiastic.

◆ Avoid too many 'fillers' (see page 191).

◆ Speak clearly without mumbling.

Activity 5

1 In groups of four or five briefly share ideas on what you think happens in a job interview. If any of you have experienced one it would be useful to share your impressions.

2 Staying in your groups, role-play some interviews for one of the jobs below. Decide as a group whether the interview will be for:

- ◆ a shop assistant at a local newsagent's ◆ a shop assistant at a local electrical shop
- ◆ an assistant at a local vet's ◆ a coach for a local U14 team (you decide the sport).

Next, each person in the group will be interviewed in turn by the remaining members of the group. Each interview will follow the same format and ask the same questions as outlined below. Use the prompts at the side to make sure you sound confident.

You need to think about what would interest the interview panel. They would be interested in where you live, your education, what your interests are, how you spend your spare time.

For the purpose of this role-play you will make this up. For example, if you haven't worked in a shop before you can still mention experience in handling money, or in talking to members of the public.

Interview format

Good morning Miss/Mr X ...

Question 1: *Could you please tell us a little bit about yourself?*

Question 2: *Tell us, Miss/Mr X, why you have applied for this job?*

Question 3: *Do you have any previous experience that we should know about?*

Question 4: *Why do you think you are the right person for this job?*

It depends on the job. If you were applying for the job of vet's assistant you would want to speak about your interest in animals. You might talk about pets you have had or television programmes you have watched.

You need to think about what qualities the job needs. For example, if you wish to coach a team it would help if you get along with people, are reliable, know about the sport and so on.

3 After each group member has been interviewed, the group will discuss each interview in turn. They should compare what each interviewee said and vote on who they think spoke most confidently. The group will then decide on the best person for the job.

4 Each person in the group should consider his or her 'performance' and think about which speaking skills should be targeted for improvement.

Using interview techniques to explore a topic

Interviews are used to select staff for jobs. They are also used in the media for a wider audience when their purpose is usually to inform and/or entertain.

A good interview depends on effective questions and interesting answers. The two are obviously connected.

Activity 6

In groups of three or four you are going to prepare and 'perform' an interview. The interviews are for a programme called: 'For 'n' Against'. The purpose of the interview is to provide the audience with *different* ideas and opinions about a particular issue.

Step 1: Decide on the issue your group will discuss. For example, it could be on:

◆ television – whether a particular programme is good or not

◆ schools – some changes that should be made.

Step 2: Working together, brainstorm the different points of view that could be explored. It would be a good idea to decide on two or three main points on either side of the argument.

Step 3: Decide the wording of some questions that will help group members to express their opinions. Cluster questions so that there are links between them. For example, if the topic to be explored was how television could be improved, then there might be a list like this:

◆ favourite programmes   ◆ unpopular programmes

◆ the difference between different channels   ◆ how television could be improved.

Step 4: Think of a series of linked questions on these points. For example, if the first question is 'What kind of programmes do you like?' then the following question needs to explore that point further. The answer might be: 'I like soaps and MTV.' A linked question would be something like 'Which soap do you like best?' followed by 'Why is that your favourite?'

Effective questions won't invite a 'yes' or 'no' answer.

Step 5: Choose one member of the group to act as the interviewer. The others will contribute answers to questions. Remember that the role of the interviewer is:

◆ to be in charge

◆ to control who says what, so that there isn't a free-for-all argument.

It will be the interviewer's job to move between the different people in the group. For example, once one person has talked about his or her favourite soap, it would be logical to ask the other interviewee how s/he reacts to what s/he has just heard.

Step 6: Spend some time trying out questions, keeping those that 'work' and discarding those that lead to poor answers. Decide on an order of questions.

Step 7: Show your interview to the rest of the class.

Step 8: As other groups perform their interviews, use the listening and note-making skills you practised in Activities 1 and 2 to note down the main points. You should be able to organise notes in two columns: 'For' and 'Against'.

Step 9: When the interviews have been completed, discuss your own performance with a partner.

◆ What did you do well?   ◆ What areas do you feel you still need to develop?

Working in groups of three or four, prepare a short assembly that could be delivered to your Year group. Your assembly should last for approximately five minutes.

The topic

Most school assemblies are based on 'themes'. Bullying, respect, caring for the environment, tolerance, poverty and being a good citizen are examples of the kinds of themes commonly explored in school assemblies. Your group will decide on the theme for your assembly.

The purpose

The purpose of a school assembly is generally to raise awareness of ideas and issues that are important to a particular age group. It is important that the 'message' of an assembly is given in a thoughtful way that makes it easy and entertaining to listen to.

How to proceed

It is important that everyone in your group makes a contribution that may be assessed.

Step 1: Planning and rehearsing

1 Appoint a chairperson and someone to take notes.

2 As a small group you should:

   a discuss the different possibilities for a theme and take a decision about which one to pursue

   b explore a range of approaches to the theme that will involve all of you and make your assembly interesting and entertaining.

   Think back to some of the dramatic techniques you used in Unit 19 and the work you did on presentations in Unit 18.

3 When you have thought of some ideas you should try them out and discuss their effectiveness.

4 You need to decide on a structure for your assembly. For example, begin with one student making an opening presentation, introducing the theme. Follow that with a brief piece of drama exploring the issue. A conclusion may involve another student drawing out the 'message' of the drama for the audience.

5 You should build on the skills you developed in Unit 18. It is very important to use language in ways that will attract your audience.

6 As you discuss ideas and rehearse, you should remember the work you did in Unit 20 on working together with other people. This stage of your work is as important as the final presentation.

Step 2: Presenting

When you have discussed ideas and tried them out, you should deliver your assembly to the rest of your class. You may need to use prompt cards for part of your assembly but you should remember the importance of establishing eye contact with your audience.

Section F ◆ Words: spelling strategies and vocabulary
Introduction

The following units will help you to:

◆ revise and develop strategies to improve your spelling

◆ revise and remember the spellings you use frequently

◆ remember and apply spelling rules and conventions

◆ investigate more difficult spellings.

First, find out how well you can spot spelling mistakes.

How well do you spell?

When drafting and redrafting, you should check through your written work regularly. One of the important things to watch out for is spelling errors.

Some students were asked to write a letter to be sent home to Year 9 parents. Read their first draft and note the words that you think are wrongly spelt. Next to each one, write the correct spelling. If you are unsure, you can use a dictionary.

Tommorow, Year 9 will be going on the school trip. Four teachers will be accompaning them. They are going to North Wales to do some geography feild work. Students will have opportunitys to buy souvenirs and gifts for their parents.

Mid-afternoon, they will walk up a mountain, wear they will complete a worksheet based on rocks. They will be able to go to the cafeteria which has a dinning area to purchase their lunchs from. They will then decend the mountain and make their way to where the coaches will be situated.

Hopefully everyone will enjoy themselfes and the trip will not be spoiled by unresponsible students.

How many incorrect words did you find? Check them against the list on the next page.

ICT This unit will help you to help yourself improve your spelling.

Activity 1 Spelling tips and rules

1 Here are some mis-spelt words from the letter on page 196, together with a list of spelling tips and rules. Write the words in your book and match each one with the tip or rule the writer should have applied. For example, **feild = c**.

Mis-spelt words

tommorow
accompaning
feild
opportunitys
wear
dinning
lunchs
decend
themselfes
unresponsible

Spelling rules and tips:

a words ending in *–sh, –ch, –x, –z* or *–s*: add *–es* to make plural

b words that end in *–f* or *–fe*: change the *f* into a *v* and add either *–s* or *–es* to make plural

c '*i* before *e* unless after *c*'

d words ending with a *–y* after a consonant: change the *y* to an *i* and add *–es*

e sound out words

f make sure you use the right prefix, e.g. *non, dis, in, un, ir* can all mean 'not'

g verbs that end in *e*: remove the *e* before adding suffix *–ing*

h watch out for homophones: words that sound the same, but are spelt differently

i watch out for silent letters

j make sure you double the right letter in a word.

2 There are always exceptions to the rules.

With a partner, make a list of words that break rules **b** and **c**. Try to find at least **four** exceptions altogether. Think of the words that you get wrong in your own writing.

Activity 2 Mnemonics

Mnemonics help you to remember spellings by using rhymes or memorable phrases:

t o m o r r o w
tomatoes on Monday or red raspberries on Wednesday
OR
t h e m s e l v e s
elves in themselves

1 Write out five mnemonics for the following words that you may come across in Science:

alkaline	combustion	predator	oxygen	friction

2 Think of five words that you often spell incorrectly. Check their spelling, then write them down. Make up a mnemonic for each so you will remember how to spell them in future.

Activity 3 Tricky spellings

Some words make most people wonder if they are correct.

Look at this list. Choose five which make you think twice. Sound them out or make up a mnemonic. Then get a partner to test you on them.

necessary	definite	knowledge	embarrass	business
surprise	parallel	height	environment	alcohol

Remember Keep a note of words that you find difficult to spell and practise them every day to help you to master their spelling.

Activity 4 Spellings in other subject areas

1 Use one or more of the above strategies to help you to learn to spell these words from Maths and History. With a partner, shut the book and test yourselves. Then talk about which strategies you used.

dimension	symmetry	perimeter
chronology	government	parliament

2 Pick three words from your work that you know you sometimes spell incorrectly. Apply one or more of the spelling strategies to them, then ask a partner to test you.

23 Investigating word origins and root words

ICT This unit will help you to learn difficult spellings by working out where a word comes from.

Activity 1 Word origins

pp.8, 10 & 17

In Unit 1 you learned how earlier forms of English, *Old English* (Anglo-Saxon) and *Middle English* differ from *Modern English* which we use today.

1 In pairs, refer back to Unit 1 and write these words in three columns according to which era you think they are from (pages 8, 10 and 17):

eom	hosen	wrooth	leofan	e-mail
housbondes	online	dore	ealdor	feores

2 Look at the list of words that have French origin on page 9. With your partner, pick out a further six words from the list below that you think originated in France. Write them out with a note about why you think this. Use the dictionary to help you.

pâté	dentist	button	ballet	leprechaun
café	accelerate	petite	carnival	yoga

3 Now with your partner, think of four further words that come from French and add them to your list.

Activity 2 Words from Latin and Greek

Knowing the origin of a word or word part is a useful spelling tool and also an aid to meaning.

Look at these Latin and Greek words. Lots of English words include them or are based on them. Think of three English words connected to or containing each one. Then check them in the dictionary to see if you were right. What other words are listed with the same root?

◆ tele = distance (G) ◆ manus = hand (L) ◆ autos = self (G) ◆ impero = I command

Activity 3 Investigating the root word

Finding the root word will often help you to work out how to spell the whole word. Often the root word has a prefix or a suffix, or even both added to it.
e.g. **en**camp **encamp**ment

1 'Photo' appears in many words. In pairs, produce a 'photo chain'. Then each spend five minutes writing down as many words as you can that have 'photo' as the root word. See if your partner has any words that you didn't think of.

2 Check the dictionary to find more 'photo' words and find out the origin of 'photo'.

3 What are the root words in each of the words below?

enthusiastically   unhappiness   prepossessing   impossibility   undesirable

Remember The root word may change its spelling when a prefix or suffix is added.

24 Using a dictionary and thesaurus

 ICT This unit will help you to check spellings and broaden your vocabulary.

Activity 1 Using the dictionary

Use a dictionary to check **what** words mean and **how** to spell them. Don't be afraid to use more adventurous vocabulary because you are unsure of the spelling.

p.69

1 In the extract from Christina Dodwell's text on page 69, the writer conjures up an exotic place. She uses these words:

iridescent	vulnerable	tranquillity	dense
enshrouded	immense	impenetrable	sultry.

2 Look at the context of these words in the passage. What do you think they mean? Write a short definition for each.

3 Now look them up in a dictionary to see how close you were to the correct definition.

> **Beware** When using a spell-checker on a computer, correct spellings will depend on what word the computer thinks you are trying to spell.

Activity 2 Using a thesaurus

How to use a thesaurus
Using a range of words with similar meanings will add variety and interest to your written and spoken language.

p.50

1 The writer of *Postcards From No Man's Land* (page 50) uses the following words. Look them up in a thesaurus and write out three alternatives to each word. Note that you will only find the root word in the thesaurus ('ache' not aching).

aching	fumbled	flung	weak	hesitated

2 Now read the text in which the words appear (page 50). With a partner discuss whether they were well chosen. Try substituting some of the words you found in the thesaurus. Which of them work? Do any of them improve the writing?

> **Remember** When using the thesaurus, check that the words you include in your writing are appropriate to the context. Ask a friend, your teacher or a parent.

Activity 3 Choosing the right words

1 Select a recent piece of your own work and choose five words that you think you could improve on. Rewrite the sentences, substituting more interesting or appropriate words, using a thesaurus to help you. Is the new version an improvement?

p.69

2 Write the first paragraph of a feature in a holiday magazine. Use Christina Dodwell's extract on page 69 as a model and describe a place you have visited. Use the thesaurus to make your vocabulary more exciting to tempt the reader to visit.

This unit will help you to remember letter patterns.

Activity 1 Letter patterns

Some words can be grouped together because each contains the same spelling pattern, e.g. **c**ouch, **p**ouch, **v**ouch, **t**ouch.

1 In pairs, think of at least three words that have the same spelling patterns as the examples below. Use the dictionary to check the spelling of the words you think of.

> com**pli**ment   h**aunt**   marri**age**

> **Remember** The letter pattern can appear at the beginning, in the middle or at the end of the word.

p.173

2 Look at Margaret Thatcher's speech on page 173, Unit 18. Find four groups of words that have a regular spelling pattern.

Activity 2 Silent letters

1 Some words can be difficult to spell because they contain silent letters. In Unit 1, Activity 5, there is a list of 'Insults about Knaves'. Write down four more words that begin with the silent pattern: **kn**.

p.13

2 With a partner, spend five minutes noting as many words as you can that contain the following silent letter patterns:

> h_____   _____gh   _____mb.

Then suggest three strategies for remembering how to spell these words. Give one example of each.

Activity 3 Complex letter patterns

Some words contain the same sounds, but are spelt differently:

◆ queue, blue, you = all have the sound 'oo'
◆ fete, late, straight = all have a long 'a' sound.

p.56

1 Look at the extract from *Stone Cold* on pages 56 and 57. How many ways of spelling the long 'i' sound can you find?

2 Look at paragraph 1 of the extract from *I Know Why The Caged Bird Sings* on page 120.

p.120

◆ Find examples of two common spellings of the long 'a' sound and two common spellings of the long 'e' sound.

◆ Write down two more examples of words which use each of these letter patterns.

> **Remember** Watch out for these varied spelling patterns in your own work.

ICT **This unit will help you to work out how words are built up and so help you to spell them correctly.**

A **syllable** is a unit of sound. Some words are monosyllabic (having one syllable, e.g. the, tree, dog). Others are polysyllabic (having more than one syllable). There is a variety of strategies you can use to help you to spell polysyllabic words.

Activity 1 Sounding out words into syllables

The words below are commonly mis-spelt in Geography. Sound them out and write them, indicating the separate syllables. Next to them, write how many syllables each one has, e.g. **atlas at – las = two syllables**.

> ◆ erosion ◆ infrastructure ◆ transportation ◆ contour ◆ estuary

Activity 2 Word shape and letter patterns

One of the strategies to learn how to spell a word is to 'visualise' it – look carefully at the shape of the word or the letter patterns within it. For example:
in **committed**
there are two 'm's and two 't's
three of the last four letters are taller.

1 Spend three minutes visualising the following words used in History, before trying to note the shape and pattern of the words.

> ◆ rebellion ◆ imperialism ◆ immigrant ◆ revolution ◆ independence

2 Now you and your partner test each other to see how many of these words you can spell correctly.

Activity 3 Words in words

We often learn to spell by dividing polysyllabic words up into smaller words or groups of letters. Try to split up the following polysyllabic words to help you remember how to spell them, **e.g. Wed + nes + day**.

> ◆ permanent ◆ technology ◆ questionnaire ◆ preparation ◆ miscellaneous

Activity 4 Looking at your own work

Now look at your own writing. Find three polysyllabic words you find difficult to spell. Check them in the dictionary to make sure you have the correct spelling. Use the above strategies to remember how to spell them.

Try to include a range of monosyllabic and polysyllabic words in your creative writing. Keep this in mind when you attempt Activity 9 in Unit 5, *Crafting stories*.

ICT This unit will help you to increase your confidence when spelling plurals and deciding when to use apostrophes.

Activity 1 Plurals

- ◆ Most words become plural by adding –s. For example, cat → cats.
- ◆ For words that end with –s, –ch,–sh, –z or –x add –es. For example, match → matches and box → boxes.
- ◆ For words that end with –o after another vowel, you should add –s. For example, video → videos.
- ◆ For words that end with 'o' after a consonant, you usually need to add –es. For example, tomato → tomatoes.
- ◆ For words that end in –y after a vowel, just add –s. For example, monkeys. For words that end with –y after a consonant take off the –y and add –ies. For example, families.

> **Remember** There are always exceptions. Some words stay the same when they become plural, e.g. **one sheep, three sheep**. Some words change unpredictably, e.g. **mouse, mice**.
> Nouns from other languages often follow different rules, e.g. **formula, formulae**. Science books will help you to research Greek or Latin plurals.

Make the following nouns plural. Use the dictionary to help you if you are unsure or research unusual plural endings.

◆ autobiography	◆ disadvantage	◆ businessman	◆ criterion
◆ cargo	◆ ox	◆ people	◆ stimulus

Activity 2 Singular/plural ownership

- ◆ When something belongs to a person or an object, use –'s, e.g. **Sam's toys = –'s because the toys belong to Sam.**
- ◆ When something belongs to more than one person or object, add –s', e.g. **All of the students' books = –s' because the books belong to lots of students.**
- ◆ When words have their own plural form **(e.g. men, children)**, put –'s at the end, **e.g. Men's shoe department.**

Copy out the following, putting the apostrophes in the correct place.

> The zoo-keepers daily routine is busy. First he prepares all the animals meals, ready to be distributed by staff. Then, he prepares for the tourists visits where he will discuss the animals habits with his listeners. Most people ask questions and the childrens observations are always amusing. The afternoons jobs include checking that health and safety rules are observed.

This unit will help you to recall the difference between pairs of words that sound the same.

Activity 1 Homophones

Homophones are words that sound the same, but their meanings and spellings are different, for example:

> ◆ there/their/they're   ◆ to/too/two   ◆ knight/night

When trying to learn the difference between homophones, look carefully at the spelling and try to find ways of reminding yourself.

a	**allowed** (meaning 'permitted')	**aloud** (as in 'say out loud')
b	**threw** (the past tense of 'throw')	**through** (meaning 'go through the door')

1 Discuss these homophones with a partner. Write each one in a sentence which makes its meaning clear.
   - ◆ board/bored   ◆ grate/great
   - ◆ course/coarse   ◆ braking/breaking
   - ◆ sites/sights   ◆ practise/practice

2 These sentences come from various units but one homophone has been misused in each one. Write them out, using the correct homophones.

> a Their were so many sparks from the fire.
> b That's the beginning of a counsel estate.
> c Knew homes for animals.
> d Instead of Manchester you could right down M'er.
> e Use the listening and note-making skills you
>   practiced in Activities 1 and 2.
> f Way up the good and bad points.

3 Write down four other homophones. Now write a four-line poem, using both versions of each homophone in its correct context. The first line could be:

> **Whether you can or you can't change the weather... .**

WORD CONFUSION

In your writing, watch out for:	could of, should of, would of, might of
when it should be:	could have, should have, would have, might have

29 Revising prefixes and suffixes

 This unit will help you to revise prefixes and suffixes as an aid to spelling unfamiliar words.

A prefix is a group of letters that is added to the beginning of the root word.

◆ Most prefixes have meaning, e.g. **post** = after.
◆ The prefix plus the root word form a new word, which has a different meaning from the root word, e.g. war/postwar.
◆ In most cases, the spelling of the root word does not change.

Activity 1 Finding prefixes

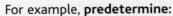

p.27

1 Look back at *Weep Not My Wanton* (pages 27–29). Find five words that begin with a prefix. For each word state:

◆ what is the prefix?   ◆ what does it mean?
◆ what is the root word?   ◆ was the spelling changed when the prefix was added?

> For example, **predetermine**:
> ◆ the prefix is **pre**, meaning **before/beforehand**
> ◆ **determine** means **to work out/make a decision**.
> **Predetermine means to determine beforehand or to work something out in advance.**

Activity 2 Antonym prefixes

An antonym is a word that has the opposite meaning to another word, e.g. **big** and **small**. An antonym prefix added to a root word creates a word with the opposite meaning to the root word, e.g. **religious**, **ir**religious.

In one column, write the following root words:

◆ legal	◆ climax	◆ stable	◆ articulate	◆ tidy
◆ cyclone	◆ worthy	◆ mortal	◆ authorised	◆ regular

In another column, write their antonyms, using the correct prefix from this list:

◆ ir–	◆ il–	◆ im–	◆ anti–	◆ in–	◆ un–

For example: **Root word   antonym**
                  legal   i̲llegal

Activity 3 Prefixes in other subject areas

In Maths or Science you may have come across words with prefixes, such as **tri**, **centi** or **micro**.

1 Write down at least eight words from Maths and Science that have prefixes. Try to use at least four different prefixes. Check the dictionary to help with the spelling.

2 What does the prefix mean in each of these words? Explain how to find out.

A suffix is a group of letters added to the end of the root word.

◆ The spelling of the root word may change, e.g. use/use**less**; pity/piti**less**.

◆ The new word will have a different meaning, e.g. fear**ful**.

◆ If the root is a verb, some suffixes will change it into a different part of speech, e.g. explode – explo**sion**; explo**sive**; explo**sively**.

Activity 4 Finding suffixes

The following are suffixes:

◆ ly	◆ sion	◆ ity	◆ ment	◆ tion	◆ ed
◆ er	◆ ery	◆ able	◆ ing	◆ ful	◆ es

p.98

1 Investigate suffixes in the text *Oleander Jacaranda* (pages 98–99). Find and write down fifteen words that use at least five different suffixes listed above.

2 Look at the words you have listed. **Did the root word change its spelling when a suffix was added?** If so, in what way?

3 How did the suffix change the meaning?

4 With a partner, think of other suffixes that weren't included in the above list.

Activity 5 Doubling consonants

Consonants are sometimes doubled when you add –*ing*, –*ed* or –*er* to the word.

> **Rule** – When a word:
>   has one syllable
>   has a short vowel sound (e.g. tip)
>   ends with a single consonant which is not an *x* or a *y*,
> **double** the consonant before adding –*ing*, –*ed or –er*
>   **e.g. chat = chatting**
>   **can = canned**
>   **big = bigger.**
>
> **Note: the consonant is also doubled on two-syllable words in which the final syllable is stressed. For example, repelled but opened.**

p.86

1 Read lines 1–11 of *Chinese Cinderella* on page 86. Note three words in which the consonant has been doubled before adding –*ing* or –*ed*. Note three words where –*ed* has been added to a word *without* doubling the last consonant. Explain to a partner why the consonant is not doubled in these words.

2 Look over a recent piece of your writing. Check all the words ending in –*ing*, –*ed* or –*er*. Apply the above rule. Have you decided correctly whether or not to double the consonants? Use the rule to help your spelling in future work.

Activity 6 Word endings

Complete the following table, adding suffixes which change the role of the word. Take care with spellings and word endings. Different words need different suffixes.

root word	verb	adjective	adverb
decide	*decide*	*decisive*	*decisively*
know			
hope			
admire			

Activity 7 Words that have both a suffix and a prefix

Some words consist of **suffix** + *root word* + **prefix**, e.g. **un**necessari**ly**.

In that example, the spelling of the root word changed when the suffix was added.

p.19

1 Below is a list of root words and a list of pairs of prefixes and suffixes. Each pair will fit round one of the root words to make a longer word. Match each root with a pair and write out the complete new word. Check the dictionary, in case the root word changes its spelling.

For example, happy + (un + ly) = **un**happi**ly** (N.B. **y** becomes **i**).

1	found	a	(in + ly)
2	stretch	b	(un + able)
3	special	c	(un + ed)
4	range	d	(im + ity)
5	dress	e	(de + d)
6	comfort	f	(out + ed)
7	possible	g	(e + ly)
8	elegant	h	(pro + ly)

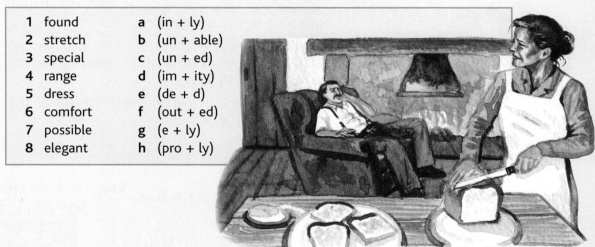

2 Work in pairs. Write down whether the new words are verbs, nouns, adjectives or adverbs.

> **Reminder** If the prefix ends with the same letter as the root word, **you don't** lose one of the letters, e.g. **un**natural or **ir**regular.

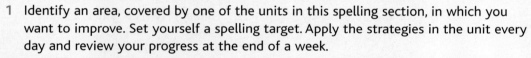 **ICT** This unit will help you to revise what you have learned about spelling.

Think carefully about what you have learned from these spelling units.

- ◆ Which are the most valuable rules and tips you have learned that will help your future writing?
- ◆ When might you use a dictionary or thesaurus to correct and improve your writing?

Activity 1 Reviewing errors

1 Use your written work from a variety of subjects to create a personal vocabulary book. Include the correct spellings of words you struggle to spell or regularly spell incorrectly. Get a friend or your parents to test you on these words often.

2 Look carefully at your recent spelling errors in at least two subjects. Are there any patterns? Learn the rules or produce mnemonics or memory aids to help you avoid these errors in the future.

Activity 2 Word perfect targets

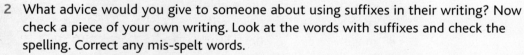

1 Identify an area, covered by one of the units in this spelling section, in which you want to improve. Set yourself a spelling target. Apply the strategies in the unit every day and review your progress at the end of a week.

2 What advice would you give to someone about using suffixes in their writing? Now check a piece of your own writing. Look at the words with suffixes and check the spelling. Correct any mis-spelt words.

3 Write out the following headlines, putting the apostrophes in the right place. Write the appropriate rule next to each.

BOYS LEG BROKEN IN 3 PLACES

ALL PARENTS VIEWS HEARD

ENGLANDS FIGHT FOR FOOTBALL TITLE

OLD PEOPLES HOMES IN DANGER

WOMENS RIGHTS

4 Think of three homophones that often confuse you. Devise three strategies that will help you to identify the difference between them and to use them in the correct context.

Activity 3 Keep checking

1 Look carefully at the last two written pieces in your History and Geography books. Are apostrophes, homophones and spellings correct? Set yourself two targets to improve your work in those subject areas.

2 Make checking fun! Exchange books with a partner, checking that they have used homophones and apostrophes correctly and there are no errors in their spellings.